JODY FISHER'S
THE ART OF SOLO GUITAR
Book 1

THE JAZZ GUITARIST'S GUIDE TO SOLO GUITAR ARRANGING

Copyright MMII Workshop Arts, Inc. • All Rights Reserved. Printed in U.S.A

Acquisition and Editorial: *Nathaniel Gunod*

Editorial: *Michael Rodman*

Music Typesetting: *New England Master Engravers* and *Timothy Phelps*

Cover, CD and interior design: *Timothy Phelps*

CD Recorded and engineered at *Studio 9*, Pomona, CA

Cover photo: *Larry Lytle*

Book: ISBN 1-9299395-53-1 • Book and CD: ISBN 1-9299395-52-3

TABLE OF CONTENTS

Track
1

A compact disc is available for this book. Using this disc will help make learning more enjoyable and the information more meaningful. The CD provides you with the sounds of many of the book's examples. Track 1 will help you tune to this CD. Have fun!

ABOUT THE AUTHOR

Jody Fisher has worked professionally in virtually all styles of music during his career, from straight-ahead and contemporary jazz to rock'n'roll, country and pop. He taught Guitar and Jazz Studies at the University of Redlands and Idyllwild School of Music and the Arts (ISOMATA). An active performer in the Southern California area, he maintains a private teaching practice and is a director of the National Guitar Workshop.

Other instructional products by Jody Fisher:

30-Day Guitar Workout
Beginning Jazz Guitar (video)
Chord and Scale Finder
Ear Training for the Contemporary Guitarist
Jazz Guitar Christmas
Jazz Guitar Masterclass
      (with Joe Diorio, Mark Whitfield,
      Ron Escheté, Scott Henderson
      and Steve Khan)
Jazz Skills
Rhythm Guitar Encyclopedia
Stand Alone Tracks: Smooth Jazz
The Complete Jazz Guitar Method:
      Beginning Jazz Guitar
      Intermediate Jazz Guitar
      Mastering Jazz Guitar: Chord/Melody
      Mastering Jazz Guitar: Improvisation
The Guitar Mode Encyclopedia
Jazz Guitar Harmony
The Art of Solo Guitar, Book 2

INTRODUCTION

You are about to embark on a journey that is both challenging and rewarding. The study of solo guitar will eventually bring you into contact with virtually every element of music. You will be striving for excellence in interpretation, arranging, taste, technique and self-expression.

For a lot of players, the experience of playing in a band is the primary goal. This is fun, and often satisfying, but playing solo can be all that and more.

Many students only want to study improvisation—but unless they play regularly with other people, their progress is slow. While there are software programs and play-along CDs that can "back you up," the experiences they provide are not equal to playing with people. Improvisation has as much to do with the musical interplay that occurs between people as the musical devices that we use. Also, students often have other obligations, such as jobs and family, which can keep them from spending the time required to see rapid progress. For these folks, learning to play solo may be a better choice.

Becoming a solo guitarist is an ongoing learning experience that will reward you with a highly personal form of expression. As a solo guitarist, you will be completely self-reliant; your skills will free you from dependency on anyone else. Also, these skills will transfer directly to group playing, so you can't really lose.

For the working pro, cultivating your solo chops can have all the same benefits with the additional bonus of creating more opportunities for employment. There will always be a need for solo guitarists. Working on this style also develops every other aspect of your guitar playing. You will end up with a better sense of melody, more control over your axe and a much greater musical perspective because as a soloist, you will also be hearing and thinking like an arranger.

This is a two-book series. Book I focuses on the nuts and bolts of playing solo guitar. Basic fingerboard knowledge and theory are covered, followed by extensive information about chords and harmony. All areas discussed are followed by music to play that will help you internalize the information you have been studying. There are sections on technique and how to harmonize a song. Developing a chord vocabulary and applying this information to your songs is a basic goal of this book.

Book 2 assumes that you know most of the information in this book and focuses on more advanced arranging techniques and adding the element of improvisation to your solo work. Special techniques such as bass lines are also covered. It is entirely possible to use all the techniques one would use in a band situation while playing solo and Book 2 will show you how. You will also find lots of information about ornamentation, the various musical and stylistic feels and many aesthetic considerations.

When studying the art of solo guitar, two areas cannot be stressed enough. First, you must always be trying to arrange your own music. The music found in these books won't be enough. You must supplement them all the time and be developing a repertoire. Secondly, you must listen to all the great masters of solo guitar. This includes all of the jazz masters as well as acoustic fingerstyle players and classical artists. There is much to learn from these disciplines.

Use this information to help you find your own voice as a solo guitarist. Have fun and good luck.

CHAPTER 1

BASIC FINGERBOARD
GEOGRAPHY

Much of your success as a solo guitarist will depend on how well you understand your instrument. You should understand the following ideas before you move on to the next chapter.

1. The guitar's six strings are numbered like this:

    The 1st string is also known as the "top" string. This makes the 6th string the "bottom" string.

    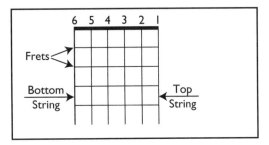

2. Playing "up" the fingerboard means moving in this direction:

    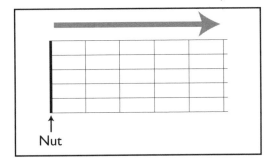

3. Playing "down" the fingerboard means moving in this direction:

    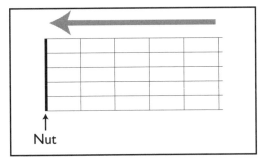

4. In standard tuning, the strings are tuned a 4th apart. The one exception is the major 3rd between the 2nd and 3rd strings.

    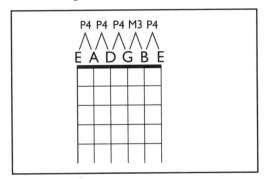

6 Jody Fisher's
The Art of Solo Guitar

5. Going from any open string to the 12th fret on that same string produces a one-octave chromatic scale. After the 12th fret, the scale repeats itself one octave higher.

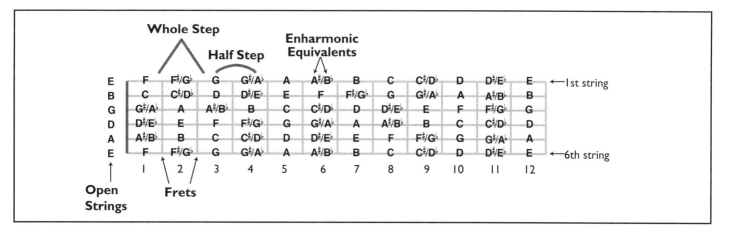

6. Any note has a unison (a duplicate) five frets higher on the lower adjacent string. The only exception occurs between the 2nd and 3rd strings. Any note on the 2nd string has a unison on the 3rd string four frets higher.

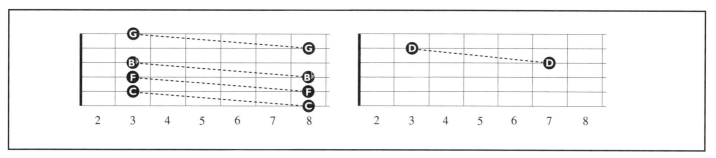

Here are some ways to help you memorize the notes on the fingerboard:

1. While away from your instrument, practice naming the notes up and down each string. For example, on the 1st string:

   E–F–F♯/G♭–G–G♯/A♭–A, and so on.

2. While away from your instrument, practice naming the notes *across* the strings at various frets.

   6th fret = A♯/B♭–D♯/E♭–G♯/A♭–C♯/D♭–F–A♯/B♭
   10th fret = D–G–C–F–A–D.

   Remember that the guitar is tuned in 4ths (except for the 2nd and 3rd strings). This bit of info should help a lot.

3. Draw a blank fingerboard chart and make about fifty copies. Fill in all the notes randomly.

Here is a fingerboard chart to use for reference. Remember that after the 12th fret, the note names repeat in the next octave (13th fret = 1st, 14th fret = 2nd, and so on).

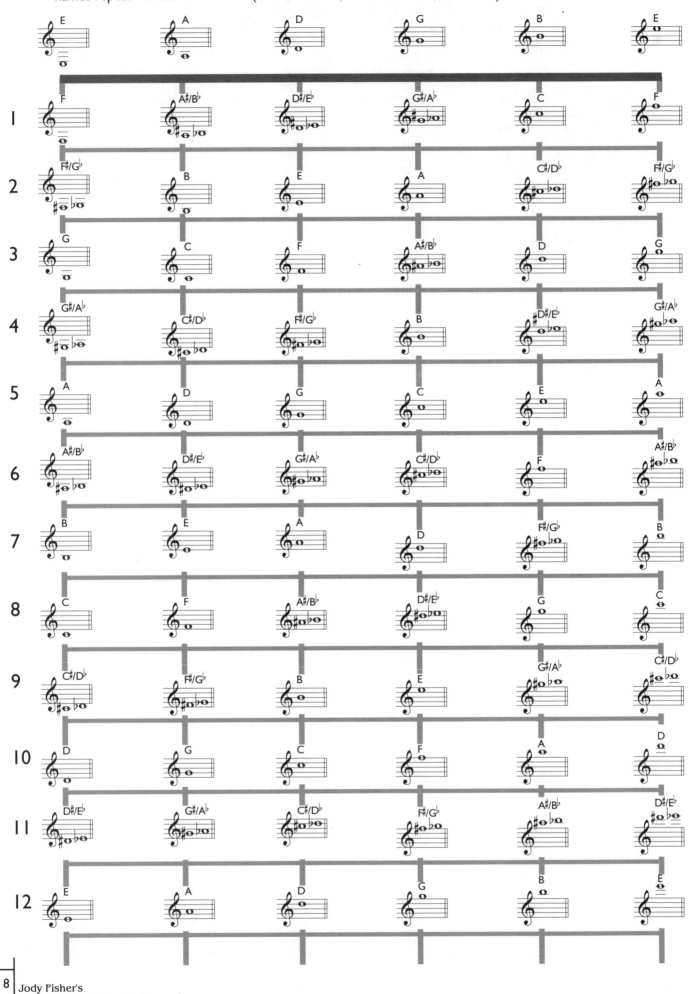

CHAPTER 2 BASIC TECHNIQUE

The idea of playing solo guitar can be intimidating—all of the sound comes from you, alone. This means that, in addition to all the theory and arranging tools we'll be discussing, you need to have a pair of hands that can respond instantly to the ideas you come up with as you are playing.

Should you play pickstyle or fingerstyle? Should you concentrate on chords or single notes? The answers are "all of the above." In order to play interesting arrangements, you need a command of many different techniques. The following section will describe some areas of technique to be conscious of when you play and practice. The exercises shown can help you on your way to more efficient hand movements. If you are interested in more information about technique, check my *30-Day Guitar Workout*, also published by the National Guitar Workshop and Alfred.

PICKSTYLE

Hold your pick between the thumb and index finger of your picking hand. How you work with your pick depends on the size and shape of the pick and the size and shape of your hand. Experiment with styles and weights. You might even want to experiment with a thumbpick. For most solo guitarists, a smaller pick is better. No matter which pick you choose, it should eventually come to feel like a part of your body.

It is very important that you learn to pick evenly. Play the following line using downstrokes (⊓, towards the floor) only. Make sure that the pick stops on the adjacent string (the 3rd string G)— think of it as a "pick stop"—and that all the notes sound identical, in terms of volume and tone. Play this a few times until it feels easy.

Now go back and play the same line again, using all upstrokes (V, toward the ceiling), and try to duplicate the sound of the downstrokes you just played. Don't worry about using a "pick stop" this time—just play naturally.

Once you have matched the sound of your upstrokes with that of your downstrokes, it is time to try picking alternately. First practice "down-up" picking and then work on "up-down" picking. Learn to listen to your own picking very carefully.

Eventually, this exercise should evolve into a rapid, but even, *tremolo* (on the guitar, this term is used to describe the rapid repetition of a note). Keep your body relaxed and your wrist very loose. Try to spend about two minutes working on each string this way.

Here is an exercise that should help you develop a smooth eighth-note picking technique. Practice this slowly at first, gradually increasing the tempo as your picking becomes more even.

This exercise should improve your triplet picking. The idea is to make your upstrokes have sound exactly the same volume and tone as your downstrokes.

Exercises 1–3 should be practiced on all six strings.

FINGERSTYLE

Playing fingerstyle allows you to create sounds and chord voicings that are not possible with a pick. Some of the ways fingerstyle compares to pickstyle are as follows:

1. In fingerstyle, we can strike all the tones in a chord simultaneously. This is a more "pianistic" sound. In pickstyle, we play one note after another, no matter how fast we strum across the strings. In addition, when we reverse the strum, we are changing the sounding order of the notes.
2. There are many chord voicings that simply cannot be played with a pick due to the need to skip too many strings. In fingerstyle, playing any combination of strings becomes possible.
3. There are certain timbres produced with the flesh of your fingers that cannot be duplicated any other way.
4. In fingerstyle, we can play walking bass lines while playing melodies and chords.
5. It is much easier to intersperse artificial harmonics throughout your arrangements in fingerstyle.
6. There are hundreds of fingerpicking patterns from various styles of music (classical, folk, jazz, and so on) just waiting to be applied to your music.

You should become familiar with the traditional names of the right-hand fingers:

Thumb	=	*p*
index	=	*i*
ring	=	*m*
middle	=	*a*
pinky	=	*c*

General Guidelines

Always keep your hand and arm relaxed from your shoulder all the down to the tips of your fingers. The success of any performance depends a great deal on minimizing tension. Keep your wrist slightly raised (or "arched") so that the tips of your fingers can "dip" into the strings. Rest your forearm, near the elbow, on the outer rim of the guitar's body. The thumb should be in front (toward the fingerboard) of the other fingers. The motion of your fingers should come mostly from the middle joints (the joint between the tips of your fingers and the knuckles). The thumb (*p*) will usually handle the 6th and 5th strings while the remaining fingers (*i, m* and *a*) are usually loosely assigned to the remaining strings.

Chords

The exercises on page 12 and 13 call upon you to practice both fingerstyle chord and single-note technique with the right hand. Play the chords using a "pinching" motion; simply squeeze the fingers and thumb together keeping your hand still—*without* the hand pulling away from the guitar. Your right hand should remain on the same plane most of the time.

Single Notes

Single notes can be handled a few different ways. Classical players usually alternate *i* and *m*. With practice, this is a very fast and accurate technique. The learning curve tends to be steep, though, so if you select this method, have patience.

Many fingerstyle jazz guitarists like to play alternating *p* and *m*. This technique produces a great "fleshy" tone. Wide leaps between strings become fairly easy and speed is usually developed more easily with this picking technique than with *i–m* alternation.

Some of the greatest guitarists in the world have used their thumbs to play single notes. You can't beat the tone once you have become proficient playing this way. For most players, though, speed becomes an issue. Once again, with practice, you may be surprised how rapidly one can play with this technique.

You will probably need to develop all of these techniques eventually. Striving for an even sound is still the most important thing—no matter how you decide to do your picking.

Turn the page to find some good right-hand exercises.

In this exercise, try to maintain a steady tempo. Switching from chords to notes (and vice versa) can be problematic for both hands. Practice slowly. Chords and notes should be played at exactly the same volume.

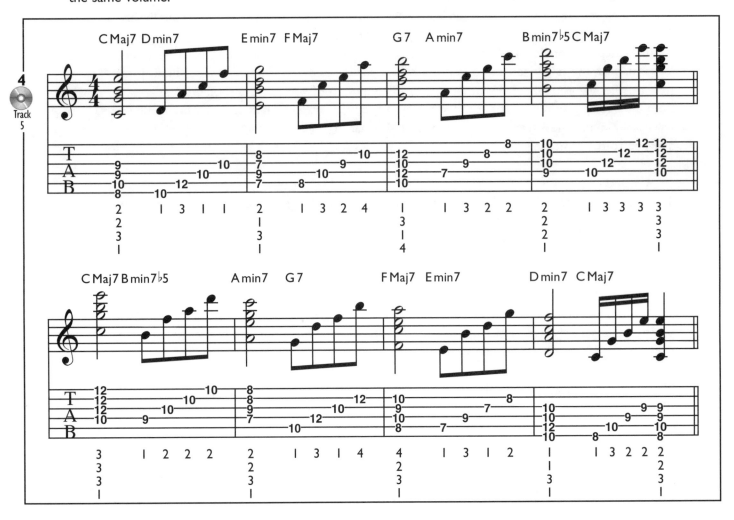

This chord exercise should help you learn to gauge the distances between the various combinations of strings. It uses what could be called an "outside/inside" pattern. Simply pluck the two outside strings (the 1st and 4th strings) together on the onbeats, and the two inside strings (the 2nd and 3rd strings) on the offbeats.

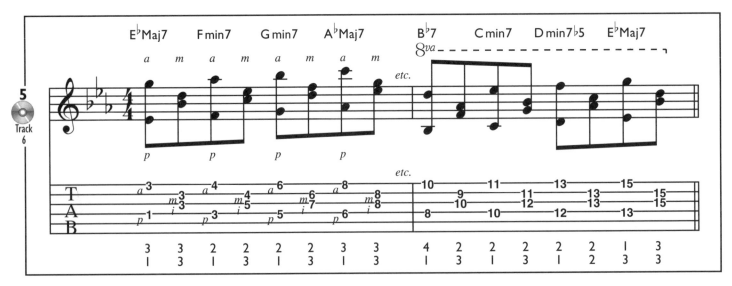

8va = Ottava. Play an octave higher than written.

Here is the same chord sequence with the right-hand pattern reversed.

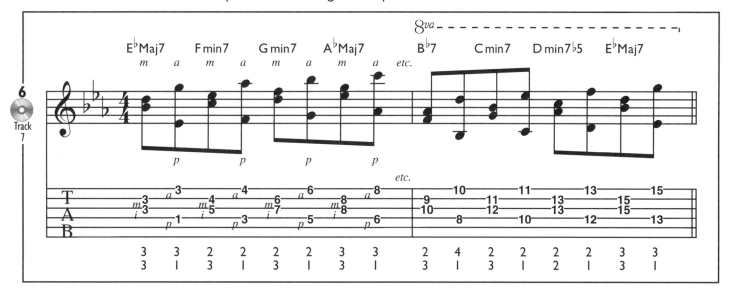

These exercises are only a starting point. Once you get started playing songs in a solo-guitar style, the areas you need work on become (sometimes painfully) obvious. At that point, it pays to look for exercises that will strengthen your particular weaknesses.

Right-Hand Summary

Some players combine elements of both pick and fingerstyle techniques. The pick is held between *p* and *i* and the remaining three fingers (*m*, *a* and *c*) are used fingerstyle. You can create some interesting sounds this way. One can also use the pick for single lines and then seamlessly switch to a fingerstyle sound for *comping* (accompanying).

It is common to combine all of the above picking elements while playing a single song. Not only does each playing style need to sound great in its own right, but you also have to make the transition from one technique to another seamless. We'll be discussing this more in Book 2 of this series.

THE LEFT HAND

There are many ways to approach left-hand technique, but a little common sense can accelerate the learning process and make playing more rewarding. Following are some ideas to think about.

Try to keep your thumb in back of the guitar neck. Wrapping your thumb around the neck creates unnecessary bends and twists in your wrist and arm. Your fingers move more easily when your arm and wrist are aligned.

Play using your fingertips only. Occasionally you will find yourself using the side of a particular finger. This is fine, but avoid using the pads of your fingers. The pads are only used to "roll" from one note to another at the same fret on an adjacent string.

Place your fingers directly behind (on the nut side of) the frets. Your job is only to hold the string against the fret, not to press the string into the wood of the fretboard. This affords the best possible intonation and requires minimal effort.

Try to keep your fingers as low to the strings as possible, rather than allowing them to stray up and away. This will optimize speed, accuracy and control.

When playing consecutive chords, be sure to let each chord sustain for its full duration. Don't hack off too much time from the end of one chord in order to get to the next one in time. When changing chords, try to lift all of the fingers simultaneously, then move them to the next position and "land" on the next chord simultaneously—think "up, over and down."

Following are some exercises to work on while thinking about the above suggestions for the left hand.

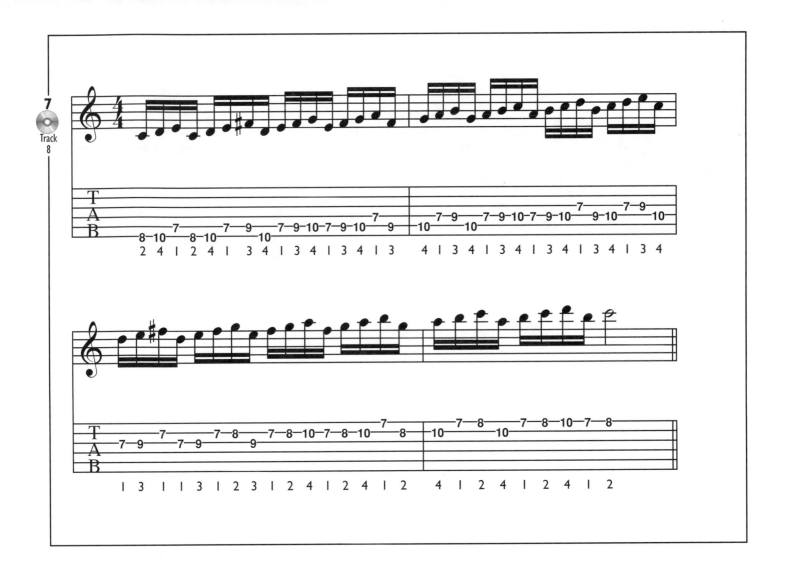

Give each chord its full value. Practice this very slowly.

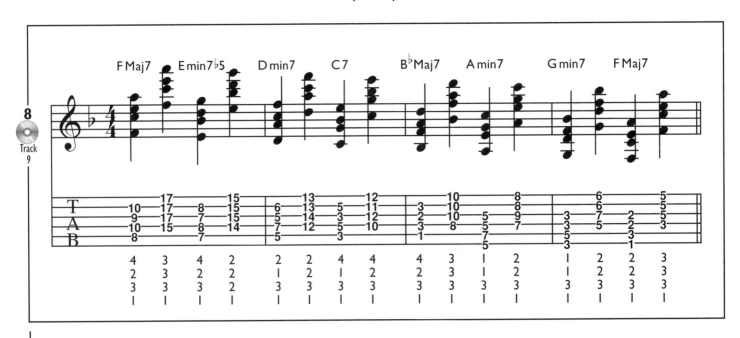

CHAPTER 3 — A BRIEF THEORY REFRESHER

We're going to talk about the basics now—just in case you may be missing some background information. It often seems as though the gaps in one's knowledge show up much more readily in a solo context.

THE CHROMATIC SCALE

Most of the music we play is ultimately based on the *chromatic scale*. This scale is twelve notes that are one *half step* (one fret) apart from each other. When the *octave* (an octave is a distance of twelve half steps) is reached the scale starts over again and so on. If you have a guitar with 24 accessible frets, your instrument has a range of four complete octaves. Below is a two-octave chromatic scale.

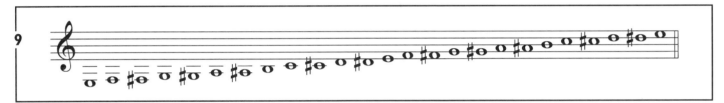

Most other scales are derived from the chromatic scale by plugging in various *formulas* (patterns of whole steps and half steps).

THE MAJOR SCALE

The formula we apply to the chromatic scale to produce a major scale is: W–W–H–W–W–W–H.

The note we start with determines which major scale we are constructing. Here is an F Major scale:

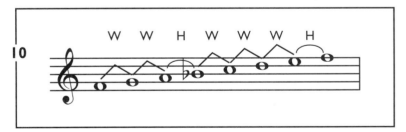

W = Whole step

H = Half step

Here is a D Major scale:

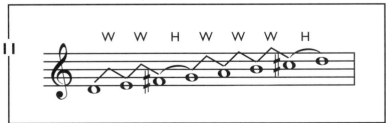

Since there are twelve notes in a chromatic scale, we have twelve possible major scales. Each major scale represents one of twelve major keys and contain different numbers of sharps or flats. Most students study these major scales in the following order: C–F–B♭–E♭–A♭–D♭–G♭–B–E–A–D–G. This order follows what we call the *cycle of 4ths* (see page 16) because these pitches are all a perfect 4th away from each other.

THE CYCLE OF 4THS

The diagram on the right illustrates many tonal relationships. In many styles of music, chords tend to move in certain patterns. One of the most common patterns is the movement of a 4th. The cycle of 4ths (or 5ths) shows this movement. The twelve keys are shown around the cycle. If you follow them around counterclockwise each root is a 4th higher than the one before it. Following them clockwise shows the *cycle of 5ths*. This is why this diagram has the two names. Some musicians like to think in 5ths and some in 4ths. Most jazz, rock and pop musicians tend to think in 4ths.

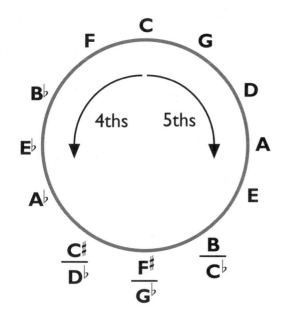

Below is a list of major scales that should be memorized away from your instrument. Thinking along the following lines should help with the memorization process.

- The C Major scale has no sharps or flats.

- The major scales F through G♭ are the "flat keys." In other words, the chromatic notes in the scale are designated with flat signs.

- As you move through the cycle, the number of flats in each scale increases by one. The 4th degree of each new scale will be the newly flatted note. That same 4th degree tells you the name of the next scale in the cycle.

- The major scales B through G are the "sharp keys." The chromatic notes in these scales are designated with sharp signs. Starting with the B Major scale, which has five sharps, each consecutive scale loses one sharp until you get to the G Major scale which has only one sharp. Once again, 4 is the magic number. The 4th degree of each of these scales will be the newly dropped sharp and the name of the next scale.

- The 4th degree of the G Major scale is C, which brings you back to the beginning of the cycle.

The Major Scales
C–D–E–F–G–A–B–C
F–G–A–B♭–C–D–E–F
B♭–C–D–E♭–F–G–A–B♭
E♭–F–G–A♭–B♭–C–D–E♭
A♭–B♭–C–D♭–E♭–F–G–A♭
D♭–E♭–F–G♭–A♭–B♭–C–D♭
G♭–A♭–B♭–C♭–D♭–E♭–F–G♭
B–C♯–D♯–E–F♯–G♯–A♯–B
E–F♯–G♯–A–B–C♯–D♯–E
A–B–C♯–D–E–F♯–G♯–A
D–E–F♯–G–A–B–C♯–D
G–A–B–C–D–E–F♯–G

THE MINOR SCALES

For every major scale, there are three corresponding minor scales, the *natural minor*, the *harmonic minor* and the *melodic minor*. They are derived from the major scale as follows:

Here is a C Major scale:

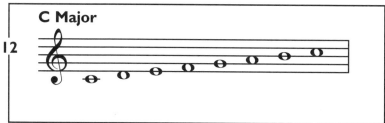

If we build a scale from the 6th degree of the major scale and progress to the octave of that note, we have created an A Natural Minor scale:

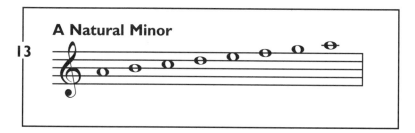

Raising the 7th degree of the natural minor scale will produce an A Harmonic scale:

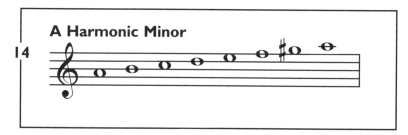

Raising both the 6th and 7th degrees of the natural minor scale gives us an A Melodic Minor scale:

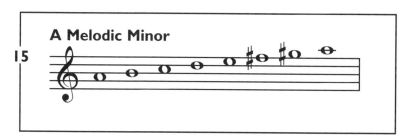

In the classical tradition, the descending version of this scale would revert back to the natural minor scale. In jazz, we maintain the the raised 6th and 7th in both the ascending and descending versions. For this reason, we sometimes call this the *jazz minor scale*.

KEY SIGNATURES

The space between the treble clef and the time signature is called the *key signature*. Here you will find varying numbers of sharps and flats. The number of sharps or flats correspond exactly to the number of sharps or flats found in a major scale. If you see four flats in the key signature, you know that the song is in the key of A♭ because the A♭ Major scale has four flats. The G Major scale has one sharp, so if you see only one sharp in the key signature you know the song is the key of G.

Since the minor scales are based on the sixth degree of the major scales, major and minor keys share key signatures. This relationship is called "relative major and minor keys".

When you see a single flat in the key signature the song is either in the key of F major or D minor because the D minor scale is based on the notes of the F major scale. Three flats would designate either the key of Eb major or C minor. You determine which it is by listening to whether the song has a distinctly major or minor sound.

Here's a list of key signatures:

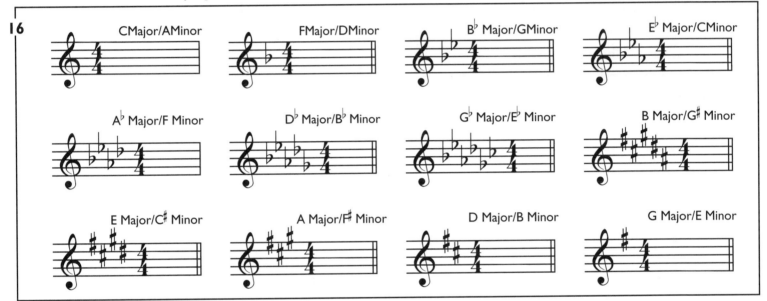

TRIADS

We are going to take a look at how triads are formed and where they appear on the fretboard. This is a big job, so take your time with this info even if you have been playing awhile. After we cover a little theory, work on the songs that follow. They are exercises that stress skills you will need for more difficult material later on.

Triads are three-note chords. Most other chords are built from triads. The four kinds of triads are major, minor, diminished and augmented, and they are constructed by applying various formulas to a major scale. The formula of a triad is a group of three numbers describing how the notes of the triad relate to a major scale built on the triad's root. For example, a "3" in a formula is the 3rd degree of a major scale; a "♭3" is the 3rd degree of the major scale, lowered one half step.

Major

The formula for major triads is R–3–5. This means we use the root, 3rd and 5th notes of a major scale to build a major triad. In the key of G, our notes would be G–B–D. In F the notes would be F–A–C.

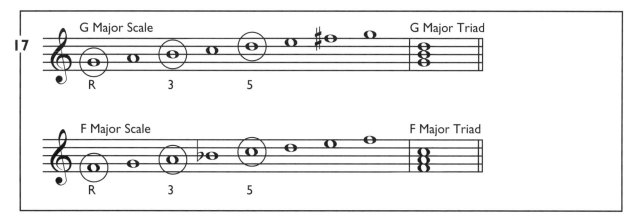

Inversions

The notes can be *inverted* to create a variation of the same triad. This is done by taking the lowest note of the triad and putting it on top. The following example shows how this is done.

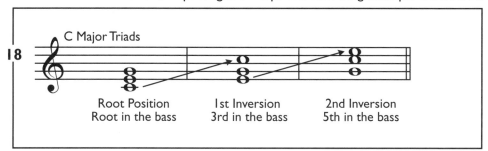

Minor

The formula for minor triads is R–♭3–5.

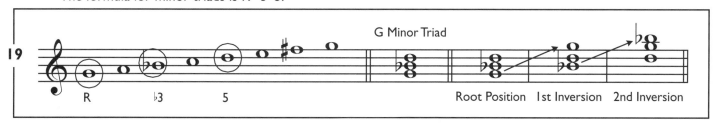

Diminished

The formula for diminished triads is R–♭3–♭5.

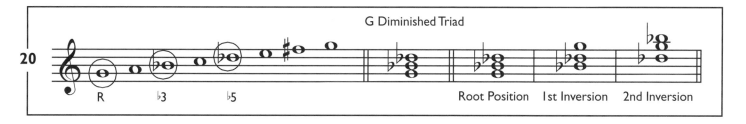

Augmented

The formula for augmented triads is R–3–♯5.

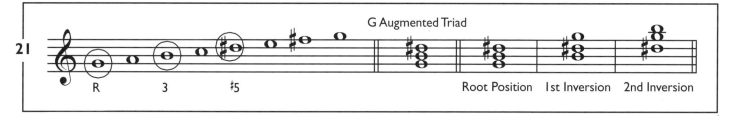

These diagrams show where the triads lie on the fingerboard. All examples are shown with a C root. Eventually, you need to be able to play all of these in all twelve keys. If you cannot do this yet, master it before continuing. It's not difficult and it will help you later on.

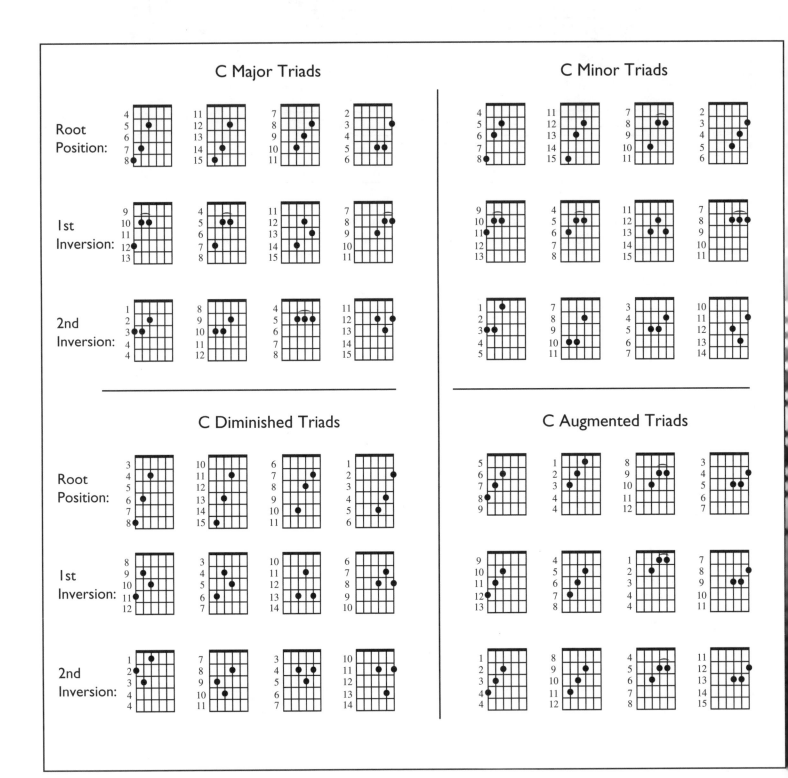

One thing to keep in mind is that the triads we've seen so far are built on adjacent strings. They're a good start, but you also need to study triads on on non-adjacent strings. These usually sound bigger or fuller because the notes are spread through the octave(s) differently. This diagram shows a variety of triads on non-adjacent strings. Once again, the root is C. Your mission is to be able to play them all in every key.

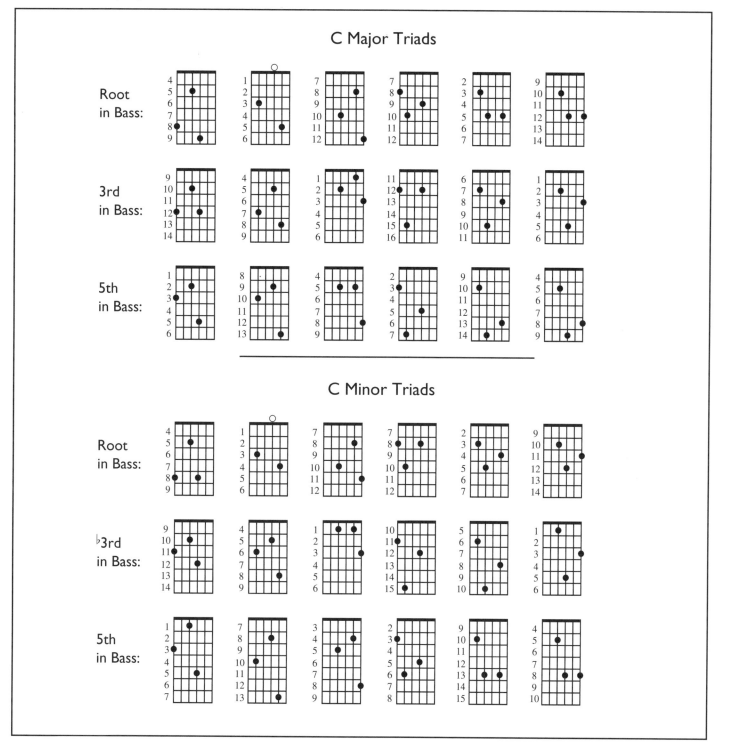

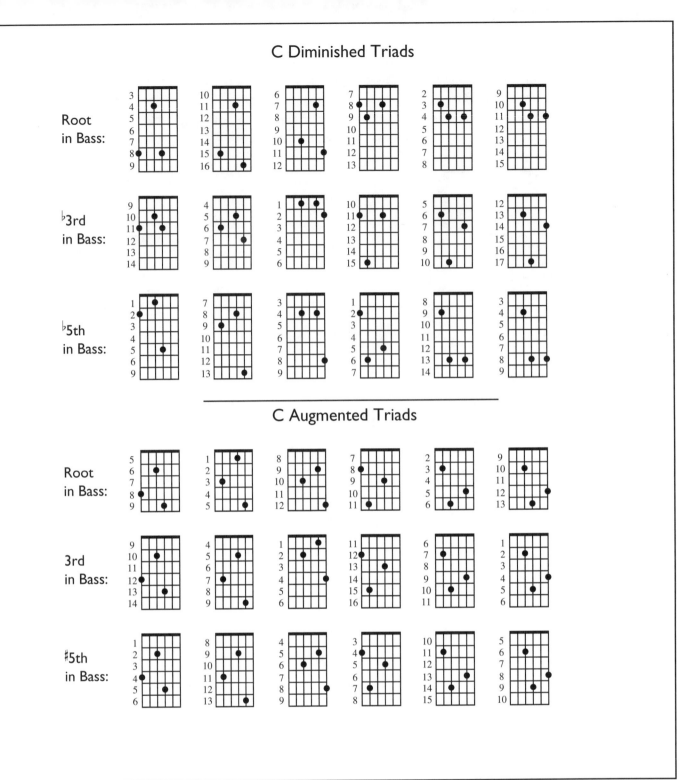

Work on the following tunes until you can play them smoothly and accurately. Play them as musically as you can. Be sure that every note in each triad rings clearly. Try to keep the single notes about as loud as the chords. This is important. You will notice that there are chords containing more than three notes. *These chords are still triads*—it's just that one or more of the notes has been doubled (or tripled) in another octave. This is common practice. The basic first-position chords most folks play when they just get started on the guitar fall into this category.

THREE SEAGULLS

SIDEWALK STRUT

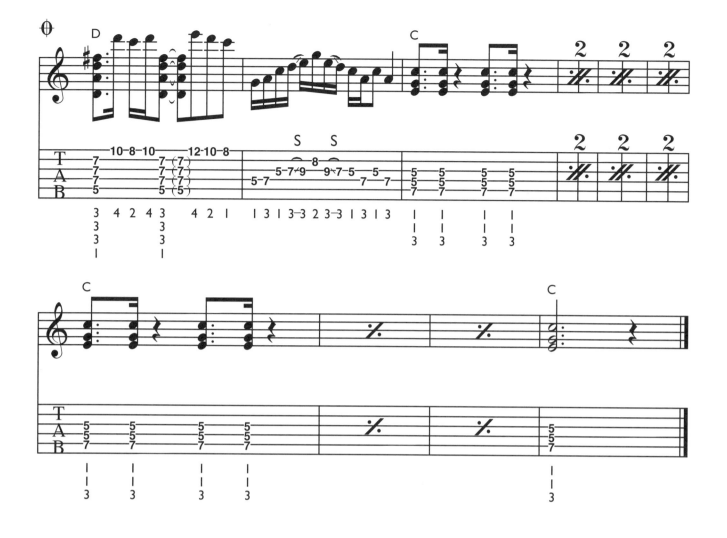

D. C. al Coda = *Da Capo al coda*. Go back to the beginning and play up until the coda sign ⊕. Then, skip ahead to the coda sign close to the end of the piece and play from there until the end.

𝄎 = Repeat the previous measure.

2
𝄎 = Repeat the previous two measures.

For the next tune, you'll need to understand the following markings:

D. S. al Coda = *Da Segno al Coda*. Go back to the sign 𝄋 and play up until the coda sign ⊕. Then, skip ahead to the coda sign close to the end of the piece and play from there until the end.

MINOR INCIDENT

DIATONIC HARMONY—CHORD SCALES

The next stop on our journey to solo guitar mastery is the subject of diatonic harmony. For our purposes, this section will help organize chord types and specific chords as well.

One way we categorize chords is by key. Let's start with triads. Here's an F Major scale:

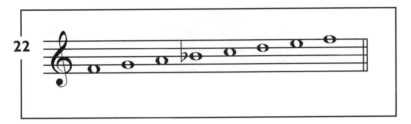

By stacking 3rds on top of each scale tone, we can find out which triads are native to the key. Below are the triads in the key of F. We call this a *chord scale*.

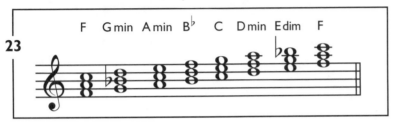

The harmonic pattern remains the same when triads are generated from *any* major scale. The pattern will always be major, minor, minor, major, major, minor and diminished. Here are examples in the keys of G, B♭ and C.

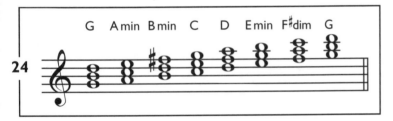

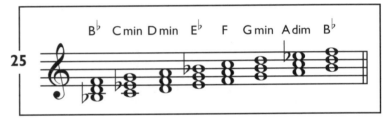

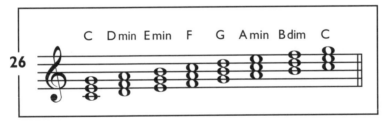

Another good way to learn triads and their relationships to each other is to build chord scales on the fretboard. We can do this moving each voice in the triad to the next note in the scale while remaining on the same string. Here is an example in the key of C:

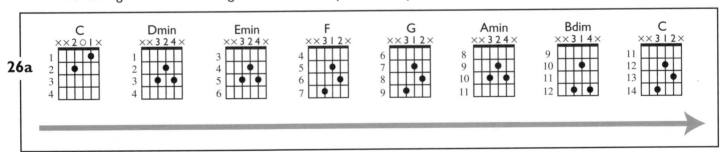

Below are twelve triad scales. Three chord-scale fingerings (one for each inversion) are shown for each string set.

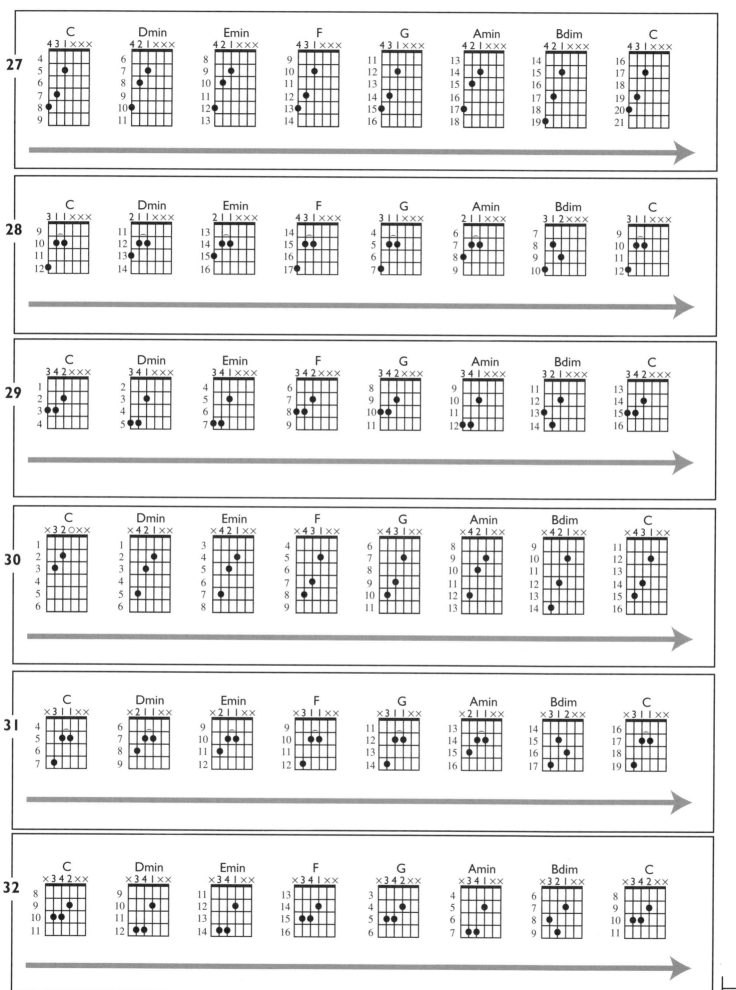

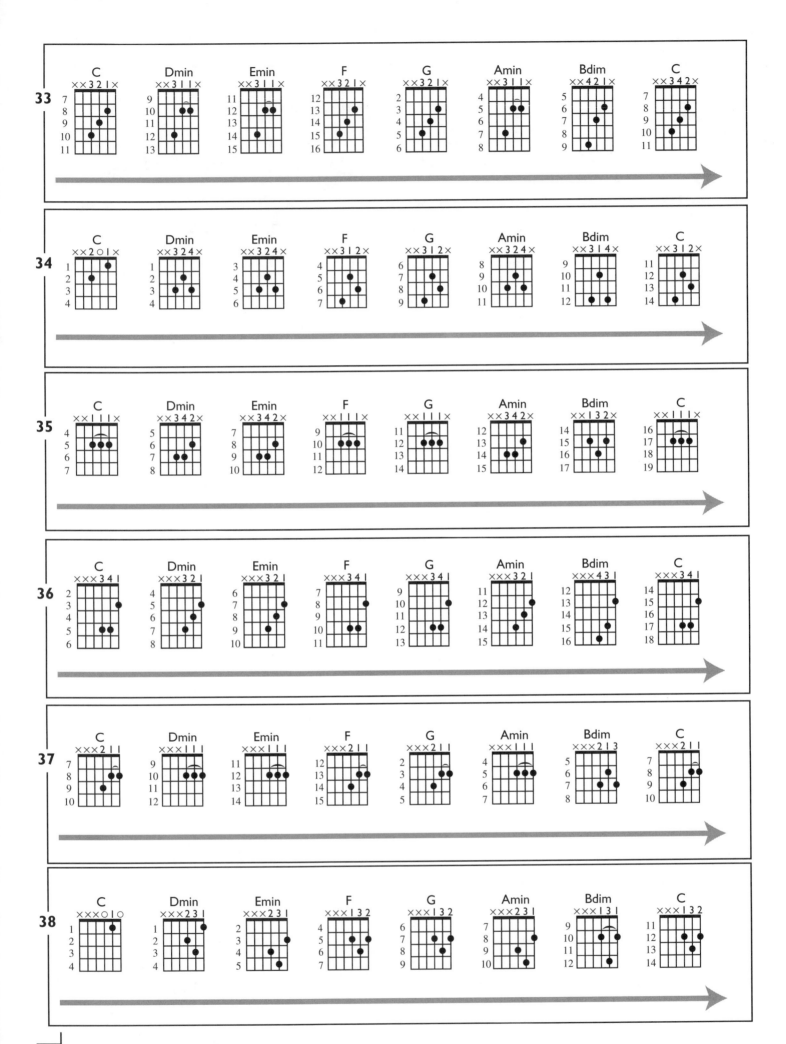

CHAPTER 4

Playing solo guitar requires that you have a command of many different types of sounds. Triads are the starting point—learning 7th chords is the next step.

7th chords are generated the same way as triads, but instead of stacking three notes, we are going to stack four. Below is an example in G.

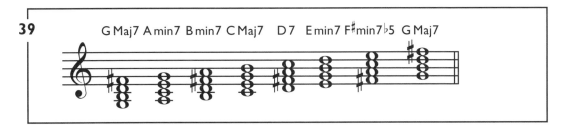

Our harmonic pattern changes a little. The pattern of chord types is now: major 7, minor 7, minor 7, major 7, dominant 7, minor 7 and minor7♭5 (half-diminished). We use Roman numerals to show a chord's position in the scale. Upper case numerals designate chords built from major triads, while lower case numerals represent chords built from minor triads. Here are a few more examples*:

Roman Numeral Review	
I, i 1	*V, v* 5
II, ii 2	*VI, vi* 6
III, iii 3	*VII, vii* 7
IV, iv 4	

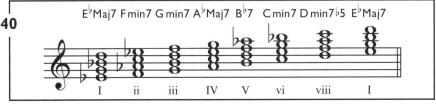

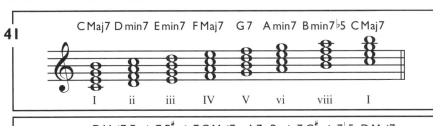

The Four 7th Chords of the Major Scale

Major 7 (Maj7) = 1–3–5–7. A major triad with an added major 3rd on top.

Minor 7 (min7) = 1–♭3–5–♭7. A minor triad with an added minor 3rd on top.

Dominant 7 (7) = 1–3–5–♭7. A major triad with an added minor 3rd on top.

Minor 7♭5 (min7♭5 or ∅7) = 1–♭3–♭5–♭7. A diminished triad with an added major 3rd on top.

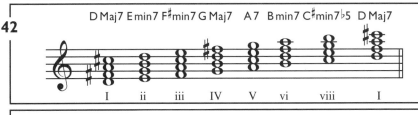

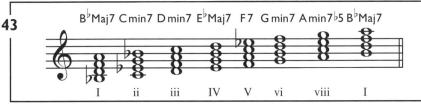

By now you should have memorized the major scales away from your guitar. It is a good idea to start saying the notes in each scale with the chord names attached. This is a good way to memorize the chords in every key. This will help you learn to transpose and will come in handy as you progress.

* When studying these examples, it is important to remember that accidentals remain in force throughout the measure in which they appear.

CHORD SCALES WITH 7TH CHORDS

Once again, let's look at some chords scales. This time, they are constructed with 7th chords.

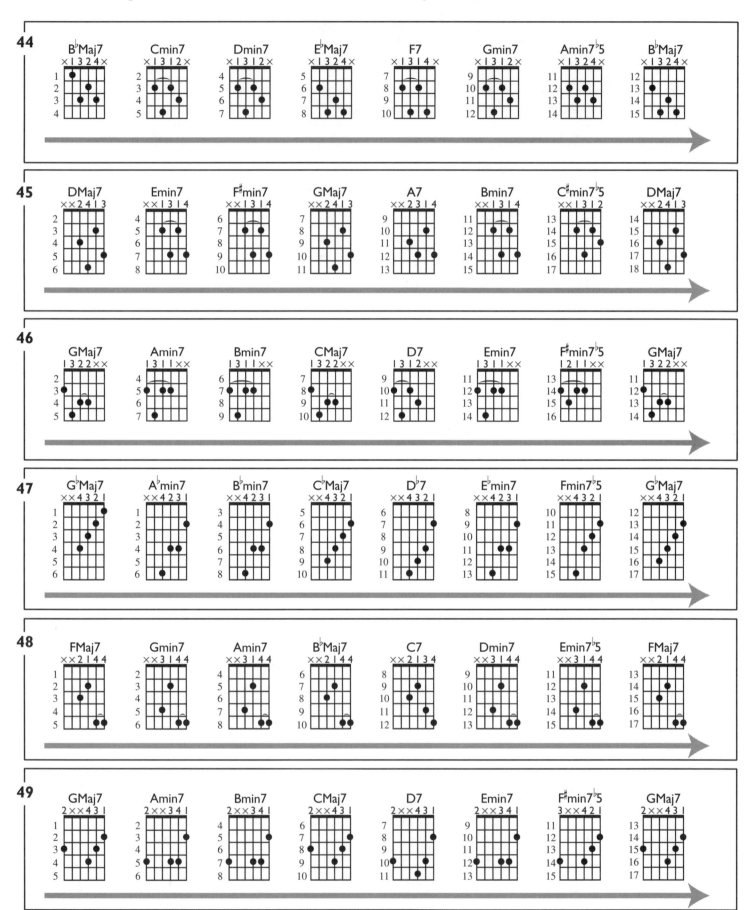

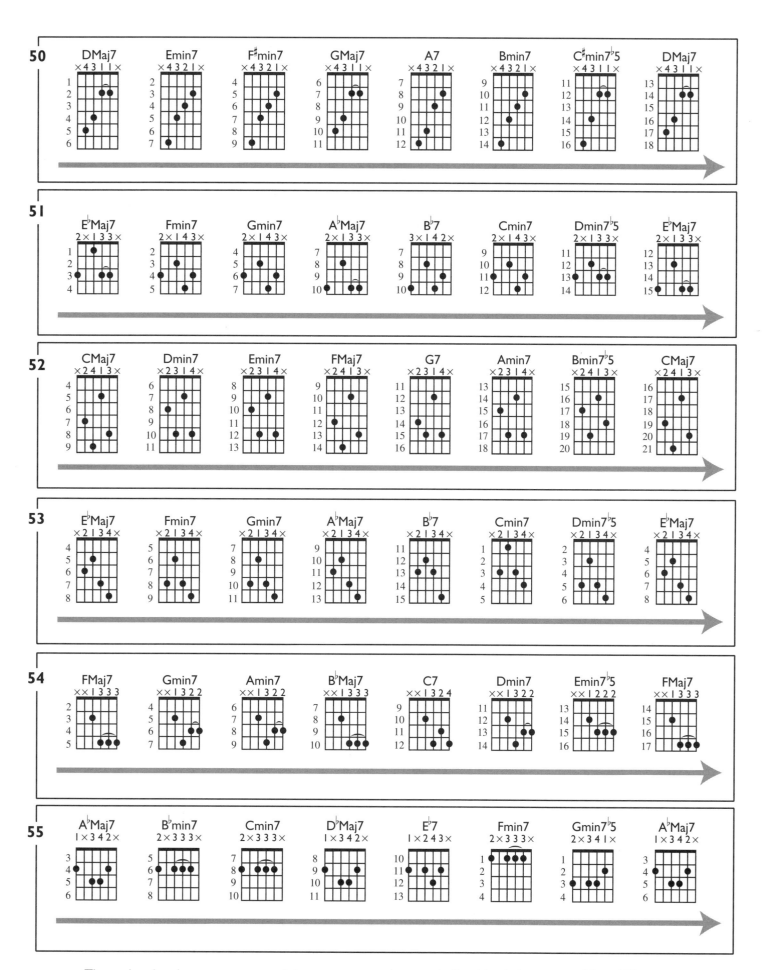

These chord scales were generated the same way as the ones built with triads on pages 29 and 30. Each voice moves to the next note in the scale on the same string. Learn these well. These chords are the basis for the music you will be working on in the next few sections of this book.

Work on the following tunes. Try to memorize the names of the chords you are playing. Maintain equal volume between chords and single notes.

MIDNIGHT IN MENTONE

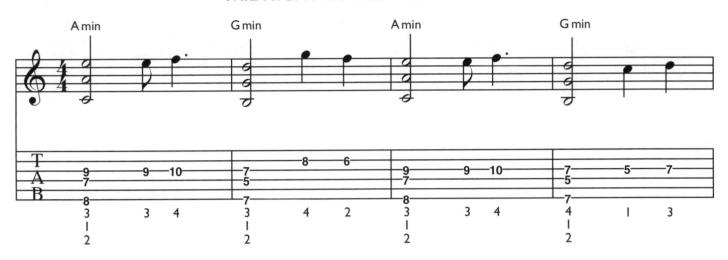

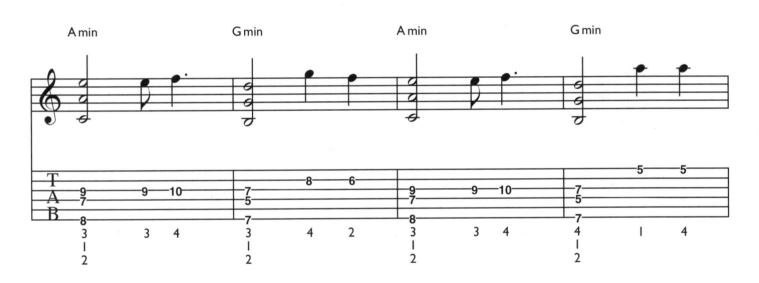

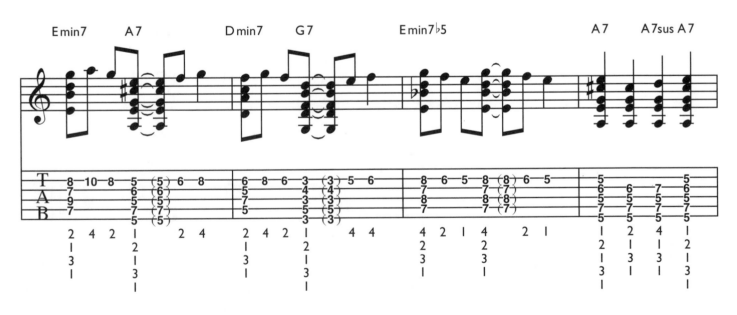

CABAZON NIGHTS

SUNSPOT

CHAPTER 5   MINOR KEY HARMONY

When we harmonized a major scale in Chapter 4, we came up with four types of 7th chords (page 31). There are more chords to use in minor keys because we combine all of the chords found in the *natural minor*, *harmonic minor* and *melodic minor* (*jazz minor*) scales. See page 17 for a description of these scales.

CHORDS OF THE NATURAL MINOR SCALE

Since the natural minor scale contains the same notes as a major scale, both scales will contain exactly the same chords. Below are the chords in an A Natural Minor scale, followed by the chords found in a C Major scale:

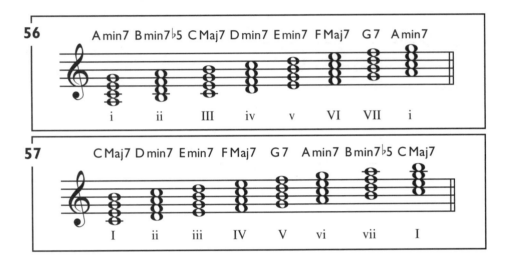

Below are some more natural minor chord scales shown with their relative majors.

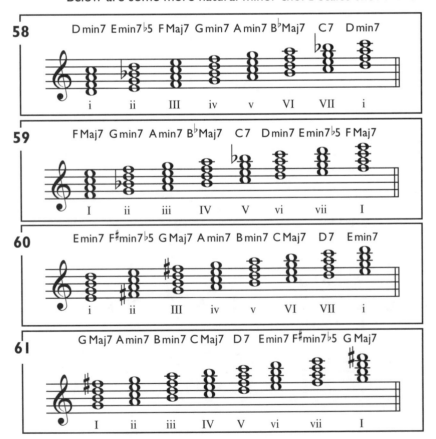

CHORDS OF THE HARMONIC MINOR SCALE

The following examples show the chords generated by the harmonic minor scale in a few different keys. In time, you should know these scales and their associated chords as well as you know the major scales and their chords. Below are the A, D and E Harmonic Minor scales with their associated 7th chords.

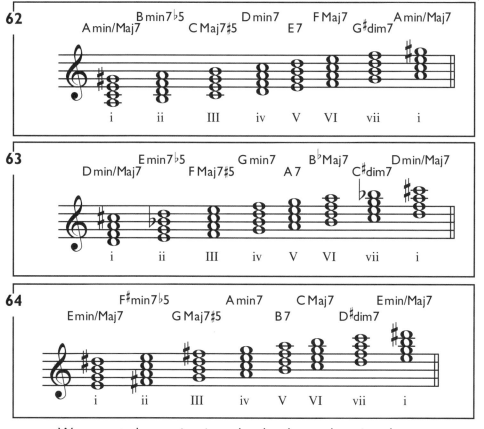

New 7th Chords in the Harmonic Minor Scale

Minor/Major 7 (min/Maj7) = 1—♭3—5—7. A minor triad with an added major 3rd on top.

Major 7♯5 = 1—3—♯5—7. An augmented triad with an added minor 3rd on top.

Diminished 7 (dim7) = 1—♭3—♭5—♭♭7*. A diminished triad with an added minor 3rd on top.

*♭♭ = *Double flat.* Lower the pitch one whole step.

We generate harmonic minor chord scales on the guitar the same way we found our major chord scales. We move each voice in each chord up one scale tone on the same string. Below are some harmonic minor chord-scale fingerings.

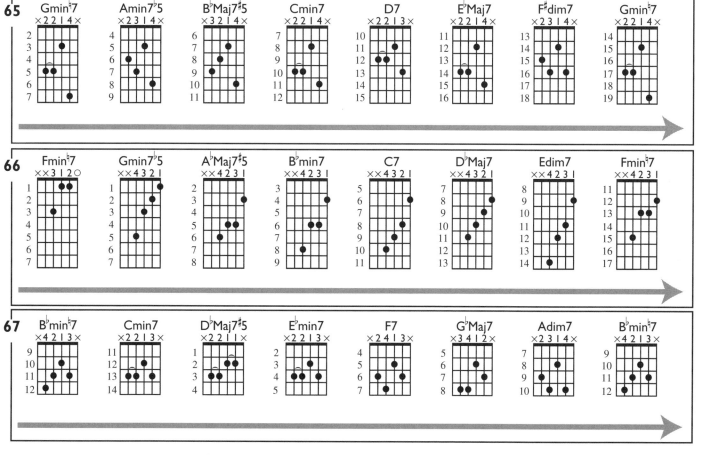

CHORDS OF THE MELODIC MINOR SCALE

Here are some examples of harmonized melodic minor scales:

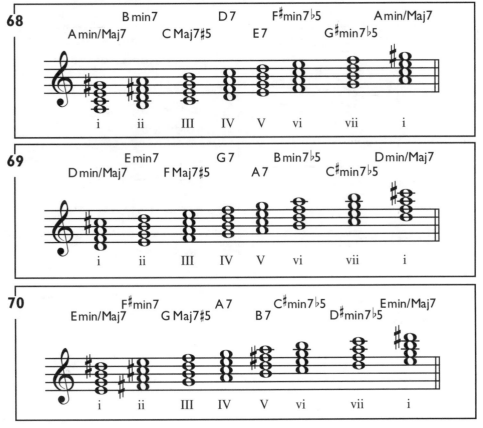

We generate melodic minor chord scales on the guitar the same way we found our major chord scales. We move each voice in each chord up one scale tone on the same string. Below are some melodic minor chord-scale fingerings.

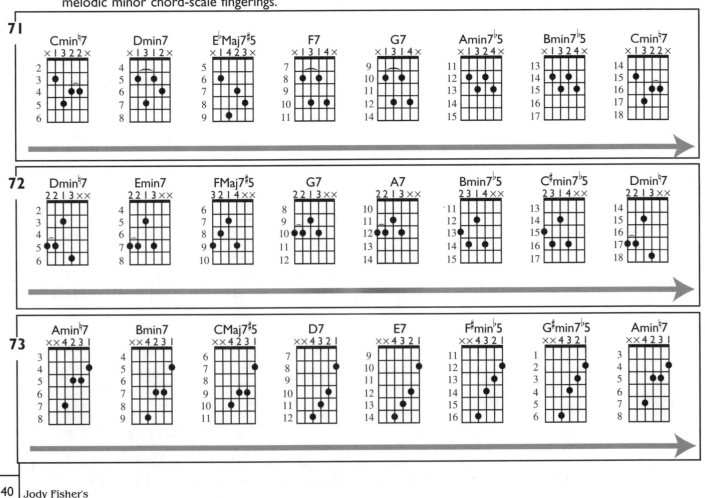

When we combine all of the chords generated from all three minor scale types in the key of A Minor, we come up with the following set of chords. You should try to memorize this information for all keys.

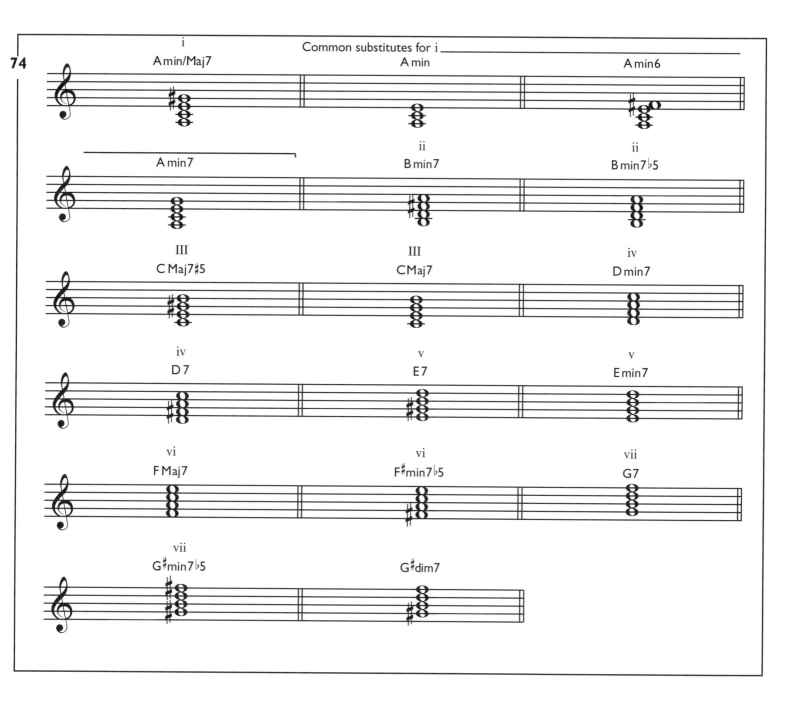

MORNING OF THE RIVER

GUIDO'S GIFT

DANCE OF THE PRAIRIE DOGS

Jody Fisher's
The Art of Solo Guitar

CHAPTER 6 — BASIC ARRANGING

HARMONIZING A TUNE

Most players eventually want to create their own arrangements. In the beginning, this is mainly a matter of learning how to harmonize parts of the melody with chords. As you progress, you will learn many harmonizing techniques as well as other ways to dress up and arrange a song. Let's start with some basics.

As you gain experience, you will come to realize that there are a lot of options when choosing ways to harmonize a melody. One of the first considerations is how harmonically dense you want your arrangement to be. Some players prefer a very sparse chordal approach, using smaller *voicings*, (a voicing is an arrangement of the notes in a chord) placed between single notes of the melody. Other players choose a thicker approach, harmonizing most of the melody with big lush chords. Still others may come up with ways to combine both approaches.

There is usually a way to harmonize any note in the melody, but we're going to start easy by finding melody notes that happen to be chord tones. Look at the following example:

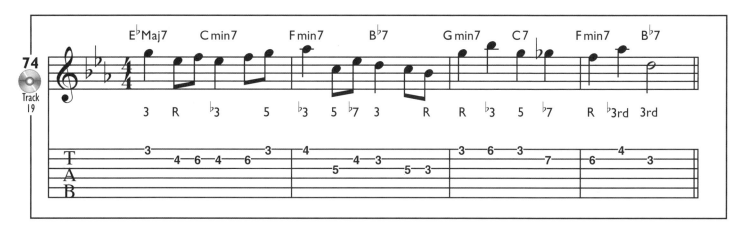

Once you can pick out melody notes that are contained in the accompanying chord, it is just a matter of scanning through your chord vocabulary until you find an appropriate voicing that will fill your need. You can see why it pays to spend time developing a huge chord vocabulary as a solo guitarist. Examples 75–78 are four different ways to harmonize example 74.

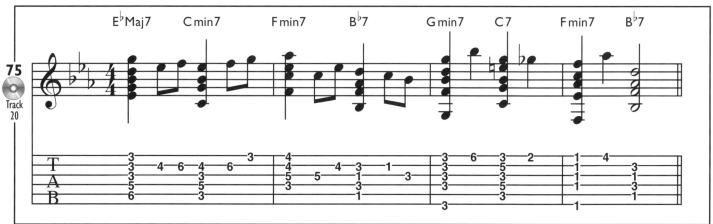

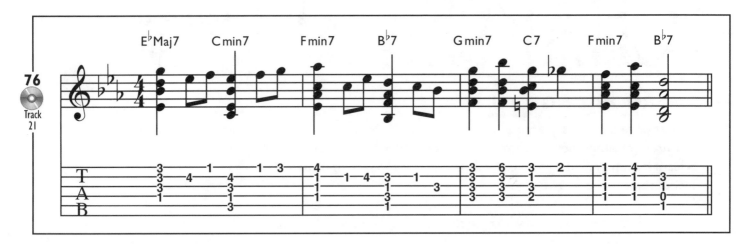

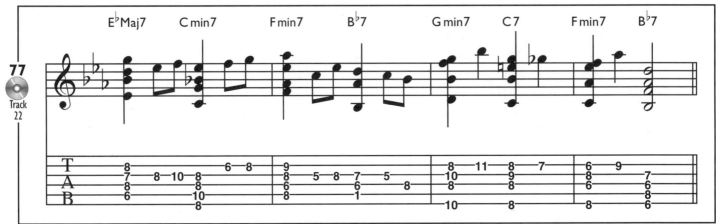

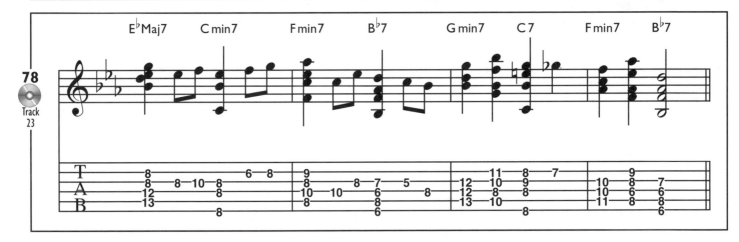

Working with chord tones only, see how many different ways can you find to harmonize the next four melodies.

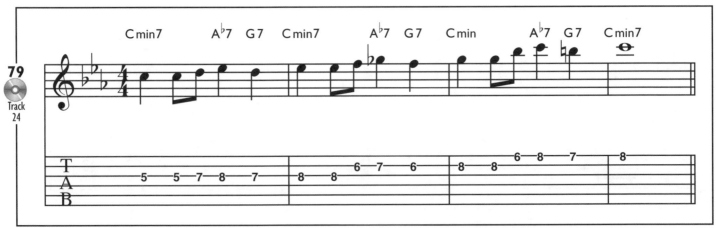

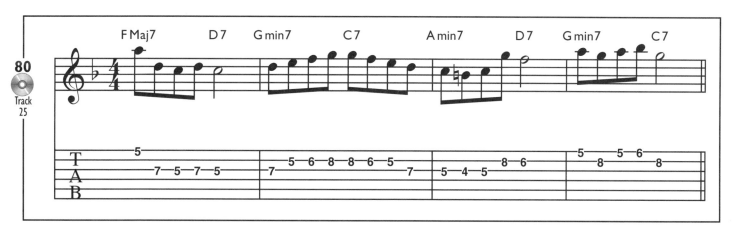

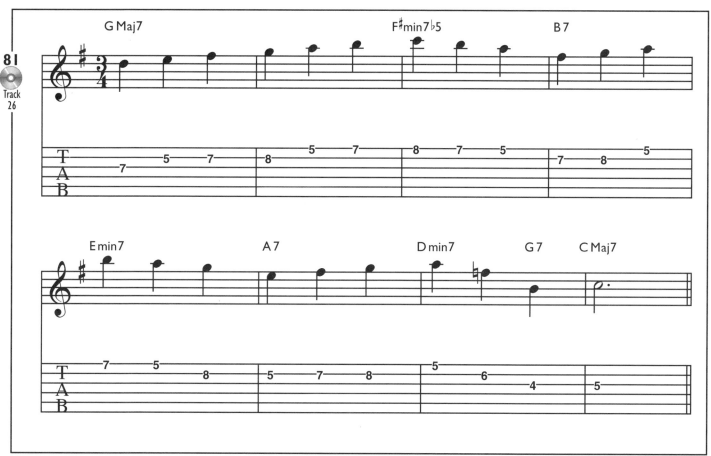

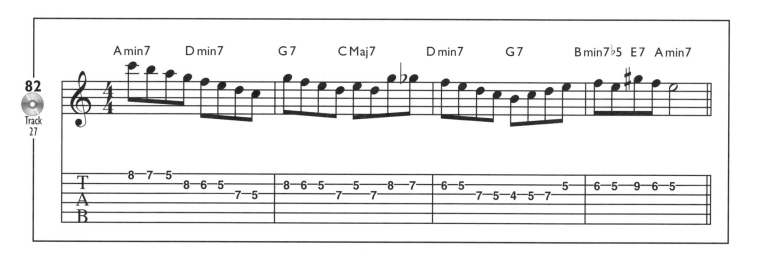

PREPARING TO CREATE AN ARRANGEMENT

There are several steps that you must take before making an arrangement. Ultimately, they will make your job much easier, although at first they might seem to be a lot of work. In time, these steps will become routine.

First, if you are basing the arrangement on the chord changes and melody found in a fake book or sheet music, you will probably raise the melody an octave. If the melody is played in too low an octave, it will be difficult to harmonize on the guitar. Raising the melody an octave usually leaves quite a few strings underneath your melody note to work with.

Regardless of what key you create your arrangement in, you should certainly know the tune in its standard key first. Besides enabling you to play the song in a group context, going through the following routine will help you understand the melody, rhythm and harmony on a much deeper level. Armed with this knowledge, your solo arrangements will sound more mature.

Step One: Learn and memorize the song's melody in single notes in all positions and octaves on your instrument. You may find that the melody sounds particularly good on a particular set of strings or area of the fingerboard. You will also find that playing the melody on different string sets suggests different chord voicings that you might not otherwise think of. All in all, you'll understand the melody (and how it lies on the guitar) a whole lot better.

This example show a few of the ways this melody can be played on the fingerboard.

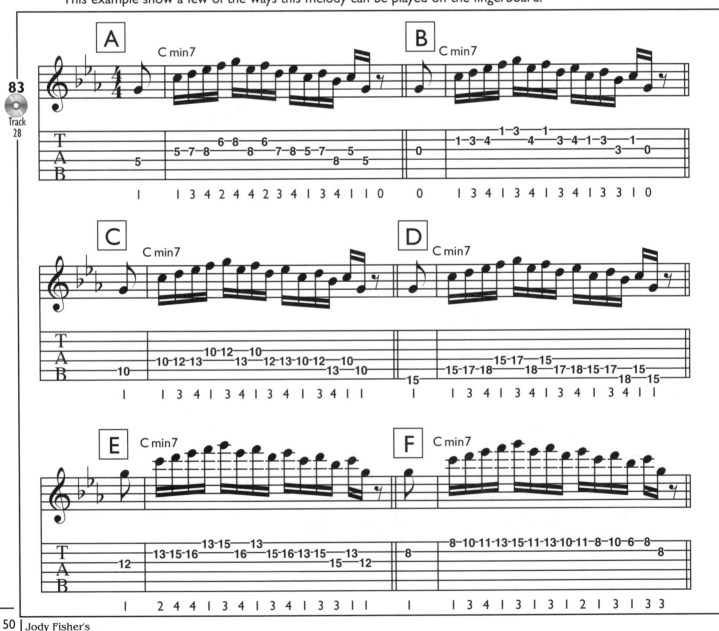

Step Two: Learn to play and memorize the song's chord changes all over the fretboard. This means methodically fencing off areas of strings and frets and being able to play the entire progression in that one area. Some possible "divisions" could include:

1. Staying on or below the 5th fret
2. Staying between the 5th and 9th frets
3. Staying between the 8th and 12th frets
4. Playing chords on strings 6–5–4–3 only
5. Playing chords on strings 5–4–3–2 only
6. Playing chords on strings 4–3–2–1 only

Of course there are plenty of options. The point is to know the harmony of the tune over the entire instrument. Later on, this will allow you to improvise with chords anywhere you happen to be on the fretboard. This will show you even more possibilities for harmonizing the melody.

Play the following chord changes anywhere you can on the fingerboard.

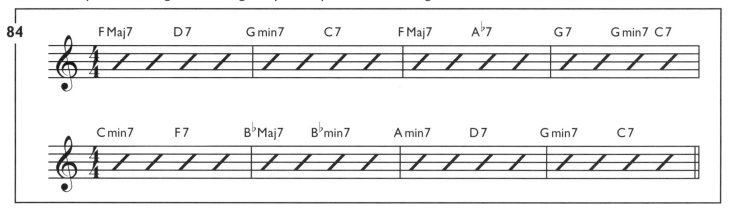

Study the following examples, which illustrate playing the chords in the various ways discussed in Step Two.

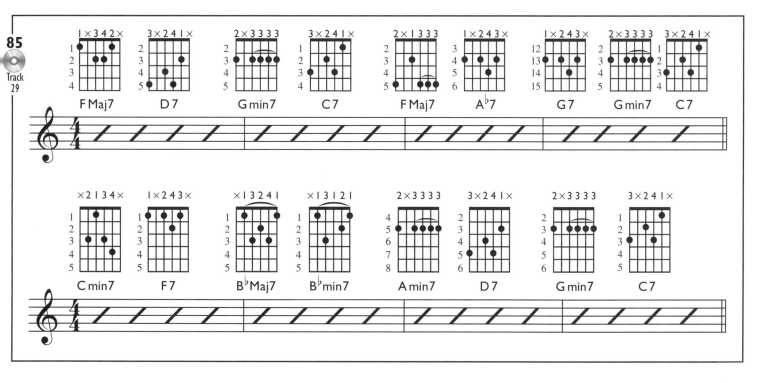

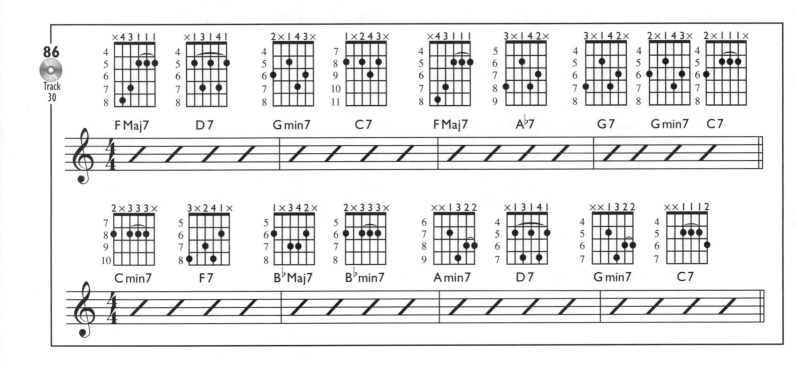

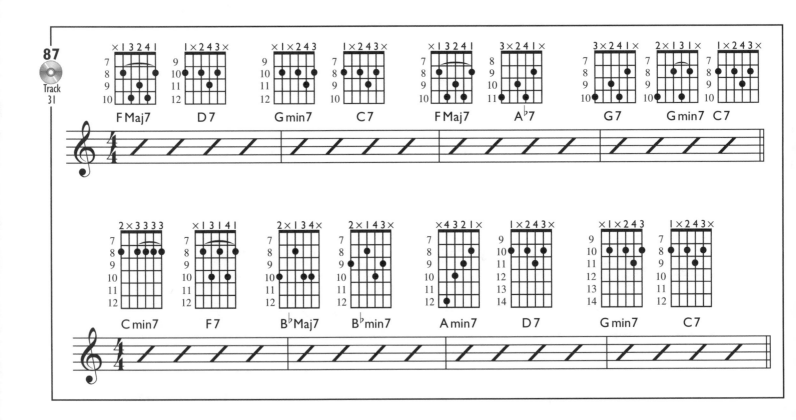

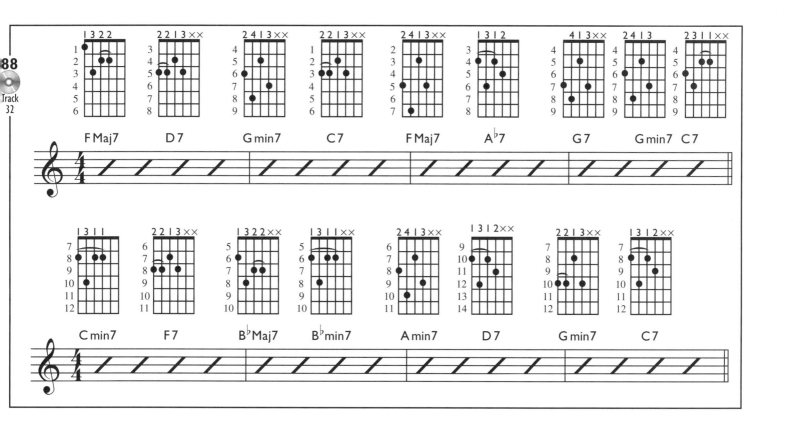

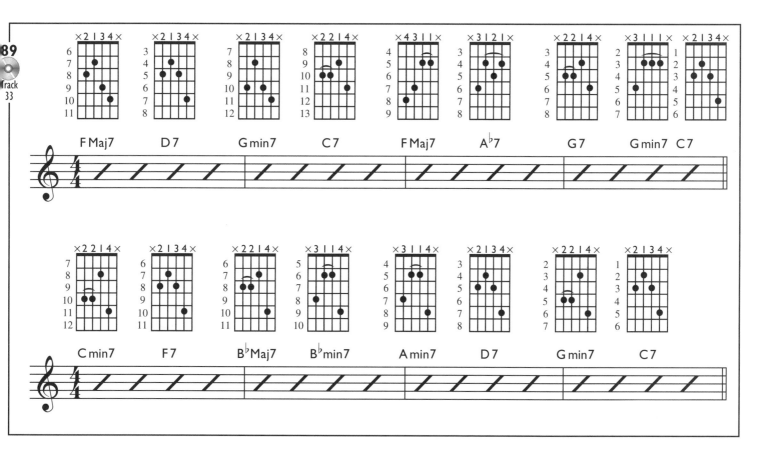

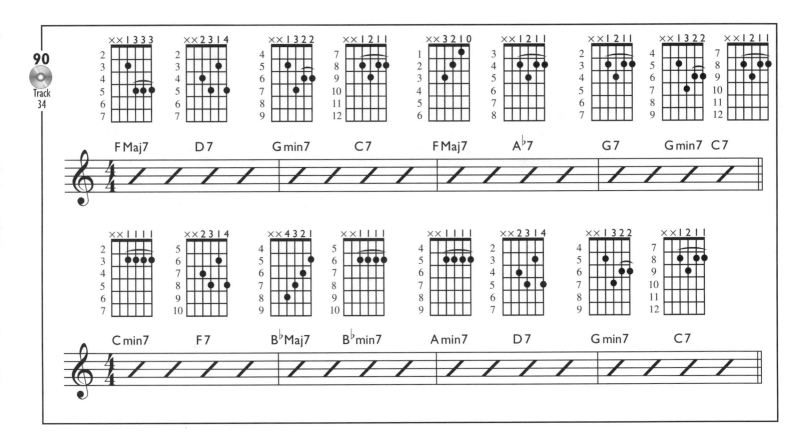

Step Three: Explore different keys to discover some of the many possibilities that the guitar has to offer. Certain keys will let you use open strings in some of your chords. This can produce unique sounds and textures. The range of some songs requires that a key change be made so that they "lie" more conveniently on the fretboard.

This short progression in E♭ sounds fine as is.

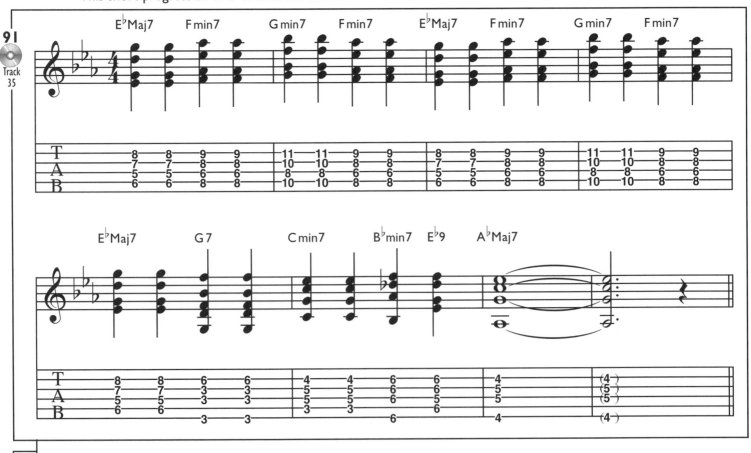

Jody Fisher's
The Art of Solo Guitar

Changing the key to E natural allows us to use the open 6th string as a pedal. This adds a little drama and utilizes one of the coolest features a guitar has to offer—a droning open string.

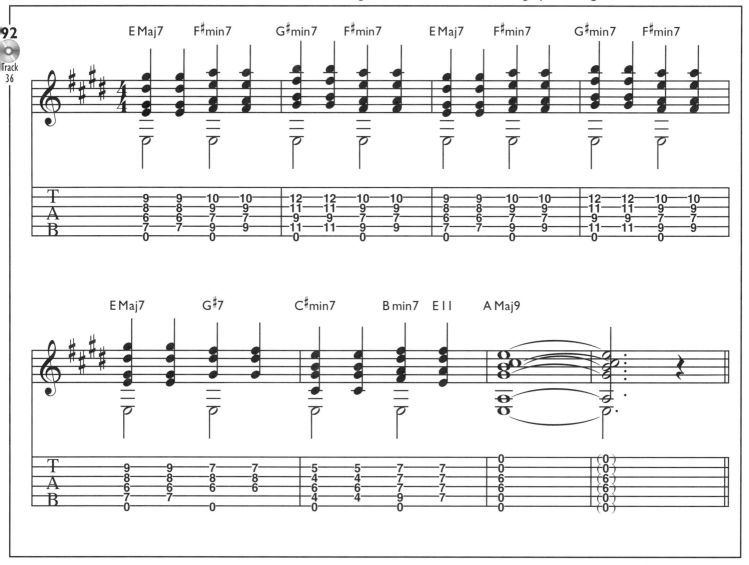

Step Four: Arrange the song with basic chords first. You'll find it easier to improvise and apply other arranging techniques later on if you have a solid blueprint of the song to work with.

Ultimately, you want to be able to improvise *everything* about the song. This keeps things interesting for both you and your audience. Being able to play a song many different ways at will is the goal. Try to keep a flexible attitude, and approach your music spontaneously. Your first few tunes probably won't feel like this, but it is important to keep these goals in mind. Your self-expression depends on it.

CHAPTER 7

PLAYING AND READING TWO PARTS

Up to this point, we have been concentrating on arrangements that have a single part. These single parts have consisted of both notes and chords in the melody. But it is also possible to think in terms of playing two separate parts simultaneously on the guitar.

When looking at written music, separate parts are usually indicated by the direction of the note stems. Notes and chords with "stems up" would be the first part while notes and chords with "stems down" would be the second part.

Learning to play this way opens the door to many possibilities. For example, you could play a melody in a higher part with an accompaniment in a lower part.

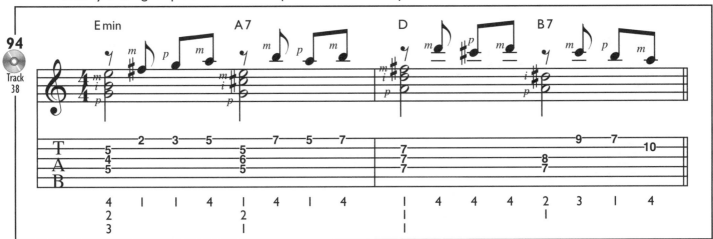

Or you could reverse that and play the melody in the bass with chord accompaniment on top.

Or you could play two separate melodies.

Two parts, each played with their own different rhythms, can create some interesting syncopation. When executed well, two-part playing can sound like two separate instruments. You can create a much larger, fuller sound and the possibilities are endless

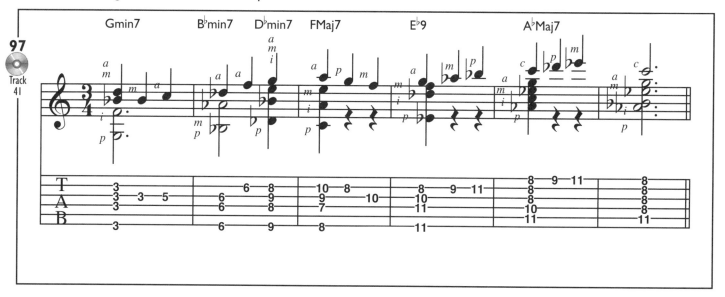

If you have never done this before, it can be tricky at first. The key is to practice very slowly, working on just one small phrase at a time until it feels easy. Then, move on to the next phrase. It is important to keep a good *balance* (the relationship between the parts in terms of volume, in this case, equal) between both parts.

While it is certainly possible to play with a pick-and-fingers technique, most players would opt for a straight fingerstyle approach instead. It is not advised to try using a pick in this two-part style.

Here are a few songs written in two parts.

THREE RAINBOWS

Jody Fisher's
The Art of Solo Guitar

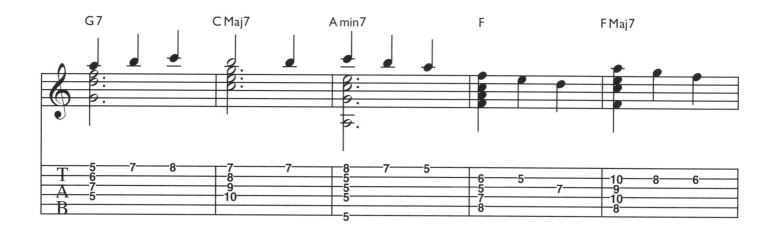

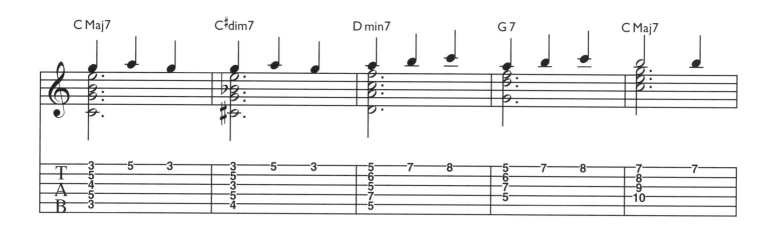

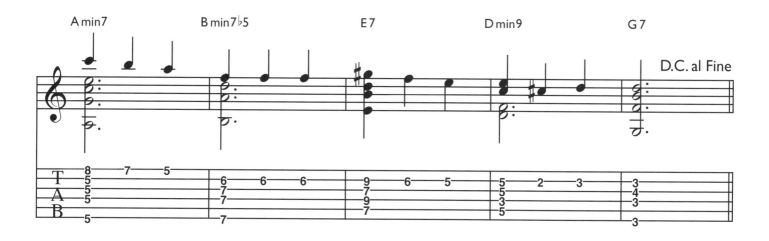

CHEAP WINE

WE'RE NOT ALONE

Try your hand at harmonizing the following tunes.

DUFFY'S HOUSE

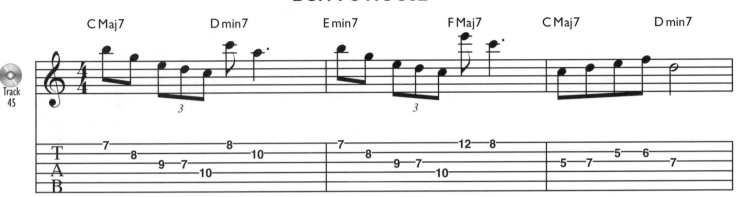

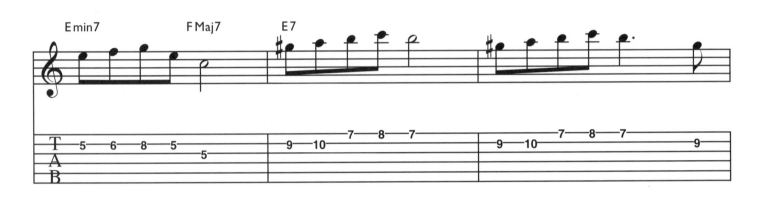

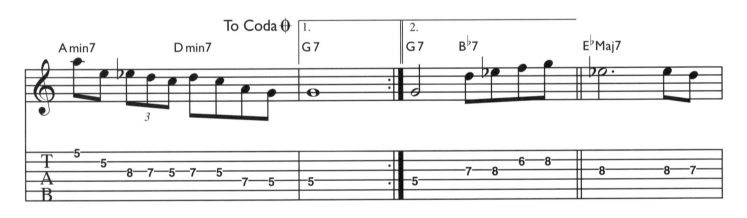

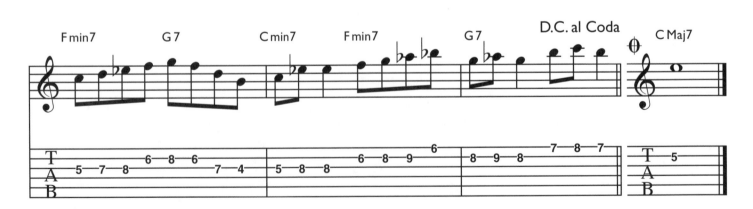

NICKEL STREET

FOUR WEEKS

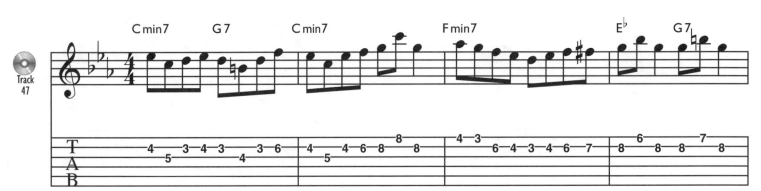

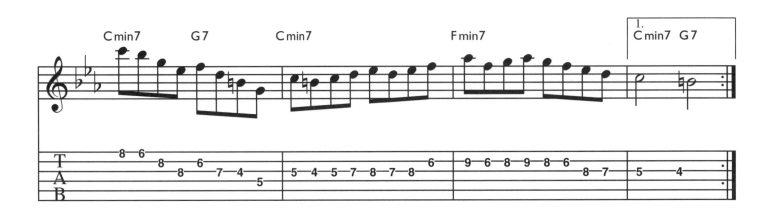

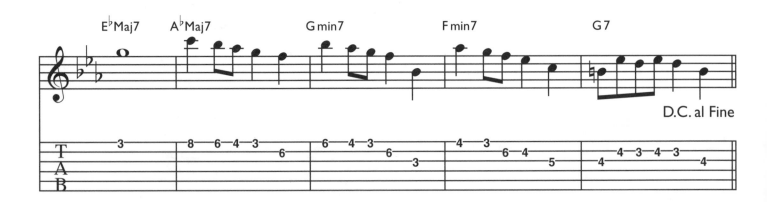

BABY, WE GOT TO HAVE US A LITTLE TALK

So far, we have stuck to basics in regard to arranging and harmony. There is much more to learn in this book and the second volume of this series. The exercises and songs you have studied on the previous pages should have been enough to give you a general idea about how simple chord/melody arrangements are written and played. Now its time to start working on *actual* tunes. Unless you are constantly working on developing your own arrangements, you cannot really progress. Each new song you learn allows you to use new information (theory, voicings, and so on) and helps to develop your skills—both mentally and physically.

There will be many more songs and exercises ahead, but your education will benefit the most from applying these concepts on your own. This cannot be emphasized enough.

You should learn all kinds of tunes. If you like jazz tunes and standards, there are dozens of fake books available with the melodies and chord changes to thousands of songs. Experiment with songs from all styles—from pop songs, to show tunes, from The Beatles to country music. In the beginning, you will be spending quite a bit of time on each tune, so be sure you like the song you are going to work on. After arranging the tune, you will be spending more time practicing it until it is ready to perform. Having songs to play will give you a context in which to apply the musical concepts you will be learning while working through this method.

So get started now. Take a break from this book and start applying the concepts you have already learned. Then come back and work on some more new material.

Joe Pass was a brilliant arranger for solo guitar. His 1973 release on the Pablo label, "Virtuoso," made him famous. He recorded prolifically for Pablo in a variety of formats: unaccompanied, with small groups, on duo albums with Ella Fitzgerald and with such masters as Count Basie, Duke Ellington, Oscar Peterson, Milt Jackson and Dizzy Gillespie.

CHAPTER 8

Using *octaves* and *double stops* in your solo guitar playing will add variety to the overall sound of your arrangements. Once you understand how they work, they're quite easy to apply.

OCTAVES

Many great players, from Wes Montgomery to Jimi Hendrix, have played melodies in octaves. Generally, the higher note would be considered the main melody, with the note an octave below adding depth and power to the sound. To a large extent, learning to play in octaves on the guitar is a visual technique. There are a few basic shapes to learn. Then it's just a matter of practice until you can skate around the fingerboard using these shapes.

This first set below is probably the most common. Use your 1st finger on the lower note and your 4th finger for the higher note. Mute the string in between with your 1st finger. This way you can easily strum through all three strings (with a pick or your thumb) and still only hear the two octave notes. Be sure to strum solidly so that it really only sounds like one note. If you are playing fingerstyle, you can play octaves by using *p* and *i*, *p* and *m* or *p* and *a*.

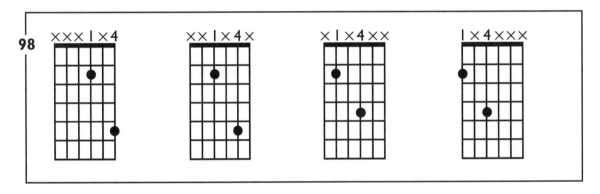

This second set of octaves sounds great but works best when playing fingerstyle because it is difficult to mute the two strings in between when playing with your thumb or pick. Finger the octaves with your 3rd or 4th finger on the lower note and your 1st finger on the higher note.

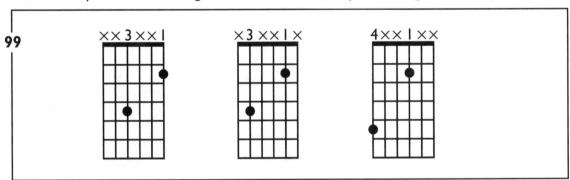

Here are a couple of common variations. This first one adds the interval of a 4th above the lower note. This is a nice effect, but be careful—it has a very distinctive sound that may not fit everywhere.

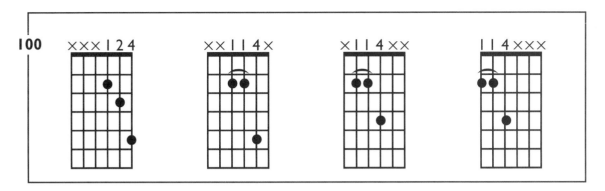

This variation adds the interval of a 6th above the lower note. Once again, be careful to use this one tastefully.

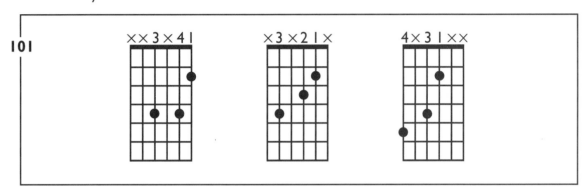

*Born in the UK in 1956, **Martin Taylor** has been influenced by Django Reinhardt and Chet Atkins alike. His powerful technique makes him an impressive solo performer.*

DOUBLE STOPS

Double stops are simply two notes played at the same time by a single instrument. They don't sound as full as chords, but they are a great way to add new sounds to your songs. Intervals of 3rds and 6ths are the most common because they tend to sound very "inside" the harmony, but keep in mind that all intervals should be practiced so that they can be applied when appropriate.

We can discover where all these double stops appear in a particular key by using the same method we used for building chord scales (page 28). Just move each note up one scale tone on the same string. The following examples show a C Major scale played in double stops based on diatonic 3rds:

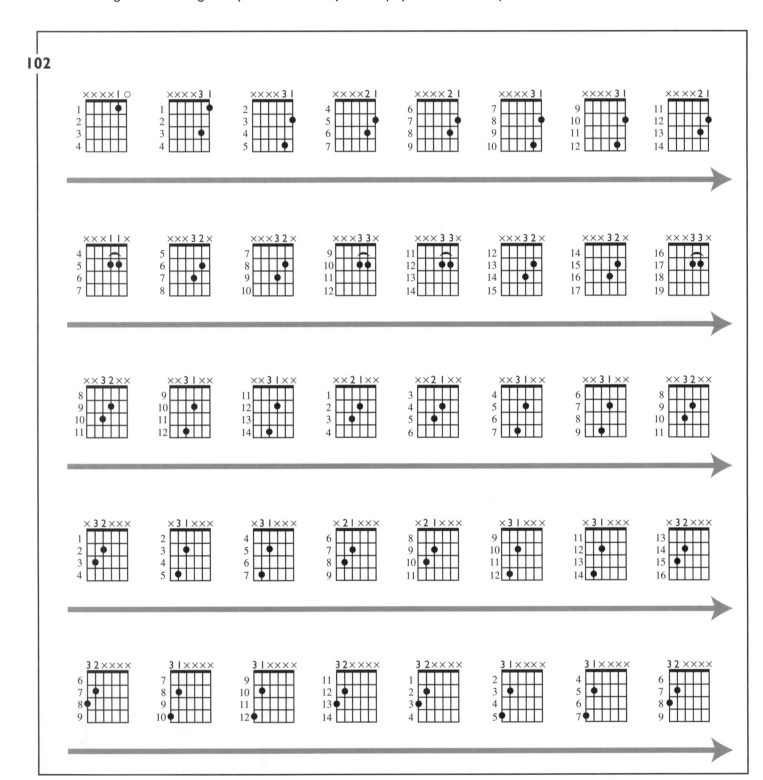

Jody Fisher's
The Art of Solo Guitar

You can also invert these shapes by dropping the top note one octave.

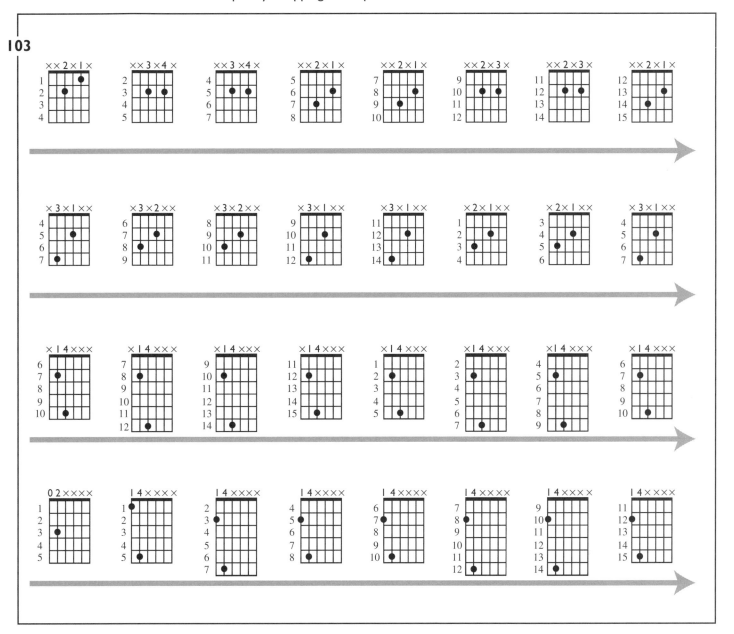

Examples 107 and 108 use diatonic 6ths above the melody notes. Transfer this to all string sets.

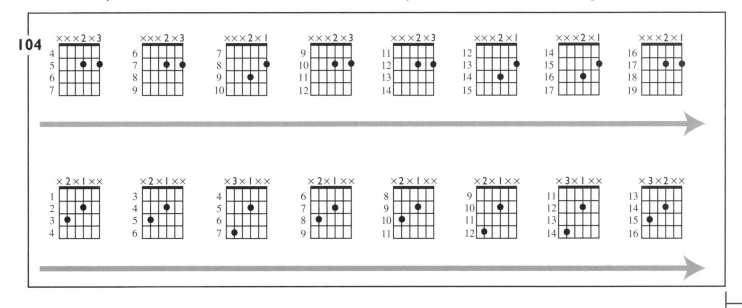

Here they are inverted:

105

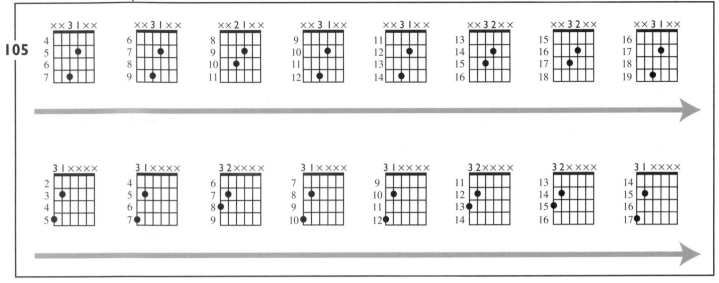

Here is an example using diatonic 4ths. Transfer this to all string sets.

106

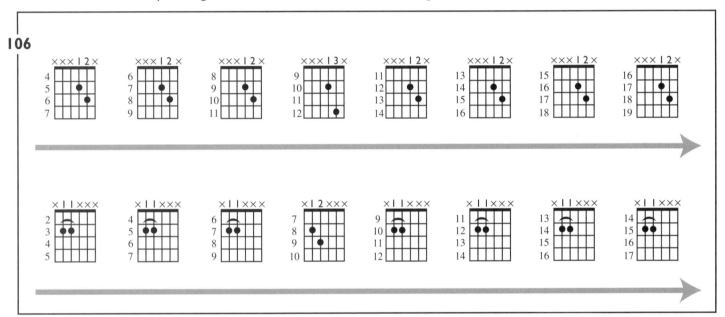

Inverted, they look like this:

107

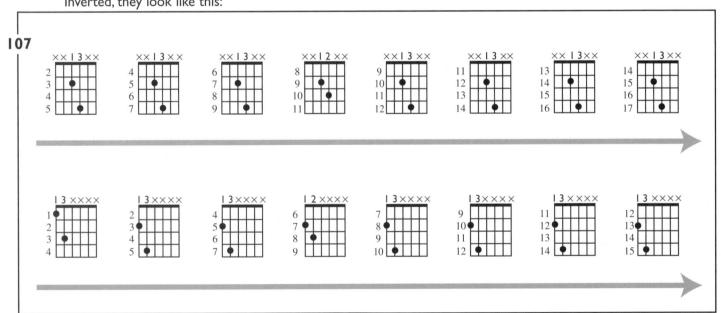

It should be noted that any interval changes when you invert it. Hopefully you noticed that inverted major 3rds became a minor 6ths, major 6ths became minor 3rds and perfect 4ths became perfect 5ths.

The easiest way to remember how inversions work is like this:

> Major intervals become minor.
> Minor intervals become major.
> Augmented intervals become diminished.
> Diminished intervals become augmented.
> Perfect intervals remain perfect.

The sum of both numbers will always equal 9. So, when inverted:

> A major 2nd will become a minor 7th (2+7=9).
>
> A minor 6th will become a major 3rd (6+3=9).
>
> A perfect 5th will become a perfect 4th (5+4=9).

Practice building double-stop scales starting from each of the following intervals. Play in all keys and on all string sets.

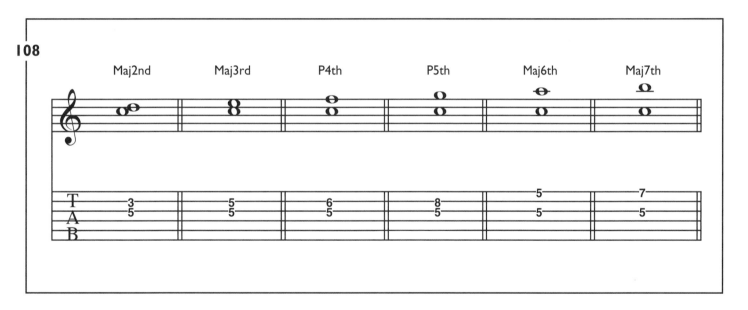

Following are two tunes that will give you some practice with octaves and double stops.

EIGHT 4 WES

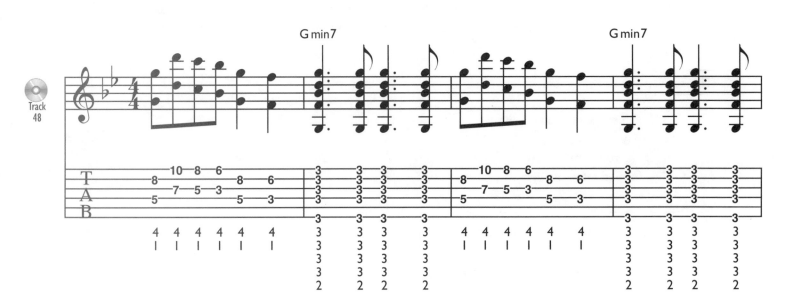

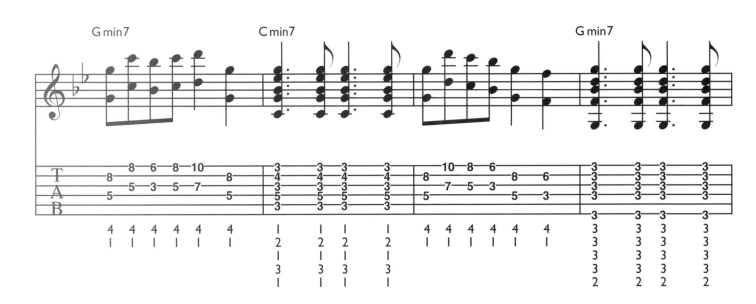

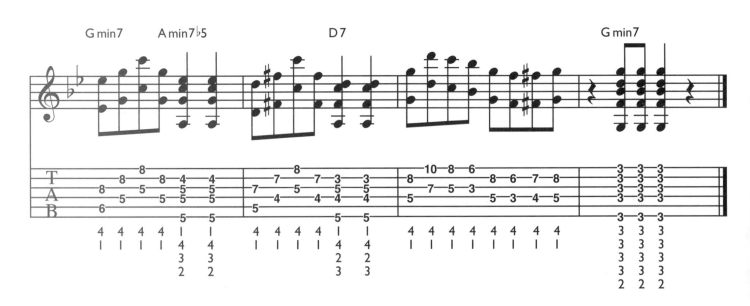

FALLING

Book 1

By this time you are probably getting around the fingerboard pretty well. Hopefully, you have become comfortable with most of the previous material and have not only learned the tunes in this book, but have worked on a few of your own as well. There are a lot of things to keep track of when playing solo guitar. All the theory, all the chord forms, technique and even just memorizing the songs themselves is quite a bit of work.

Now there are two more areas that will need attention. The first is learning to bring the melody to the forefront of the arrangement and the second is learning to keep good time.

BRINGING OUT THE MELODY

Some players are so busy thinking about the arrangement, or where their fingers are supposed to go, that they actually forget to *listen* to themselves. This is very common, especially if you are working on all the skills that are required to play good solo guitar for the first time. It can feel overwhelming, but eventually moving around the fingerboard and interpreting songs will become second nature.

Listen to make sure that the melody notes of the chords you are playing are the loudest notes in the chords. These are the notes that make the song recognizable, so you have to be certain that they are being heard. This is just a matter of being aware. When playing with a pick, try to use the higher adjacent string as a pick stop. This usually makes the highest note in the chord a little bit louder. If the melody is on the 1st string, flick your wrist upward slightly as you arrive at that string. This will help emphasize the string more.

When playing fingerstyle, it is just a matter of emphasizing the note by striking the string a little harder with the appropriate finger.

This is important. Listeners want to hear the melody more than anything else. If the tune has lyrics, they may even be singing to themselves. If your melody is the same volume as the rest of the chord, or softer, it has the same effect as a band that is drowning out the singer. So, starting listening to yourself. Listening to a recording of yourself playing can be brutal, but it is a very helpful thing to do. Once you hear it, you'll know exactly what to work on and whether your melody is coming out strong enough.

KEEPING GOOD TIME

Very few of us are born with perfect time. Most of us tend to rush or drag the tempo a little. Once again, fixing this situation is mostly a matter of staying aware of it. You could start practicing with a metronome or drum machine. Some players have been known to turn their metronome on for a few hours while at home. While this does not provide much pleasure in the way of background music, some claim it helps them develop a steady time feel. Remember that the goal is to be able to end the song at the same tempo you began it, with no fluctuations in between. This is *very* difficult, but it is a skill that can be cultivated. To help your rhythmic development, play with others that have better time than you whenever possible.

We are about to take another leap into world of chord theory. We started with triads, which gave us some basics to work with. Then, in Chapter 4 (page 31), we went on to 7th chords, which added quite a bit of variety to our chord vocabulary. The next step is creating even larger sounding chords by learning about *chord extensions*. When you stack more 3rds on top of a 7th chord, you have an extended chord.

The most common extensions we add are the 9th, 11th and 13th. We can find these extensions by looking at a two octave major scale:

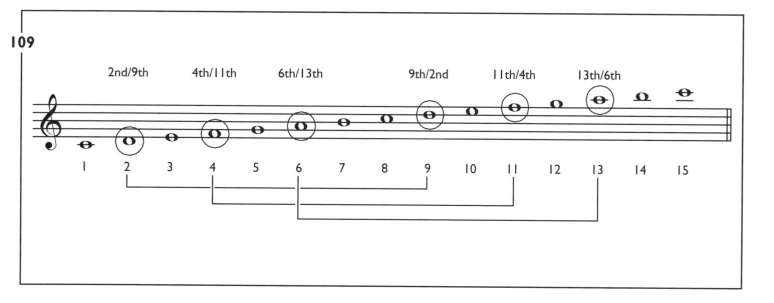

You can see that the 9th is the same note as a 2nd, but an octave higher. In the same way, the 4th and the 11th are the same note an octave apart. The 6th and the 13th have the same relationship.

One of the beauties of playing solo guitar is that you can decide to enhance or simplify any chord you want, any time you want. The more chordal options you have, the more colors to you have to work with. This is one way to keep all of your songs from sounding the same.

CHORD FAMILIES AND SUBSTITUTION

Most improvising musicians think of chords as belonging to one of three large families: major, minor or dominant. There are chords that do not fall neatly into any of these families, but they become easy to keep track of when all of your other chords are categorized.

The main idea is that chords within a family can be freely substituted for each other. We just need to make sure that the substitution chord does not contain any note that clashes with the melody of the song.

When you harmonize a note in a song that is not contained in a triad or 7th chord, you can to check to see if it could be an extension of that chord.

The following chart hows how all of these extended chords are related. The chart includes altered dominant chords, which we will discuss in the next chapter. We will use C as our root throughout. The bold chord represents the family, and the chords underneath are the chords in that family.

The Chord Familes

C Major

C6	CMaj6/9
CMaj7	CMaj7/6
CMaj9	Cadd9
CMaj13	

C Minor

Cmin6	Cmin13
Cmin7	Cmin/Maj7
Cmin9	Cmin7/11
Cmin11	

C7 (dominant)

C9	C7$\sharp$9
C11	C7$\flat$5$\flat$9
C13	C7$\sharp$5$\sharp$9
C7$\flat$5	C7$\flat$5$\sharp$9
C9$\flat$5	C7$\sharp$5$\flat$9
C7$\sharp$5	C9$\sharp$11($\flat$5)
C9$\sharp$5	C9$\sharp$5
C7$\flat$9	

There are many ways to voice any of these chords. Harmony is a lifetime study. If you are always discovering and learning to work with new chords, your arrangements will reflect this growth as time goes on. The next section explains the formulas for these chords and shows four voicings for each.

Be sure to analyze all the voicings by comparing them to their formulas. We often omit notes when forming these chords on the guitar and you need to be conscious of what notes your chords contain. Most chords should contain a root or 5th, but either one may be dropped. 9ths are commonly dropped in larger chords (11th or 13th chords) as well.

Start off by memorizing (and transposing) as many voicings from each section as you can and try inserting them in all the songs you're working on. This type of experimentation takes a little time. Have patience. Remember—just because using a particular chord may be theoretically correct, it isn't necessarily going to sound great in every situation. You will have to spend some time working with this idea on your own before you develop a sense of what works and what doesn't.

9TH CHORDS

110 Major add9
R–3–5–9

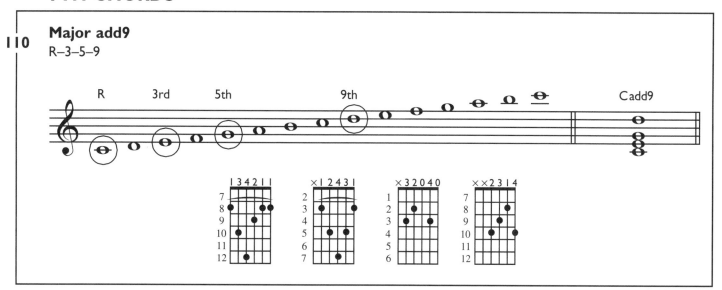

111 Major 9th
R–3–5–7–9

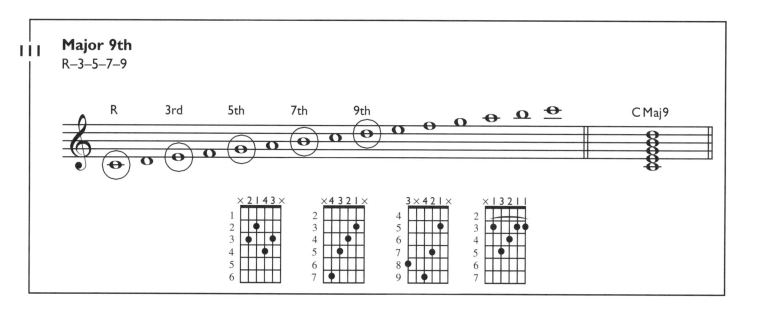

112 Dominant 9th
R–3–5–♭7–9

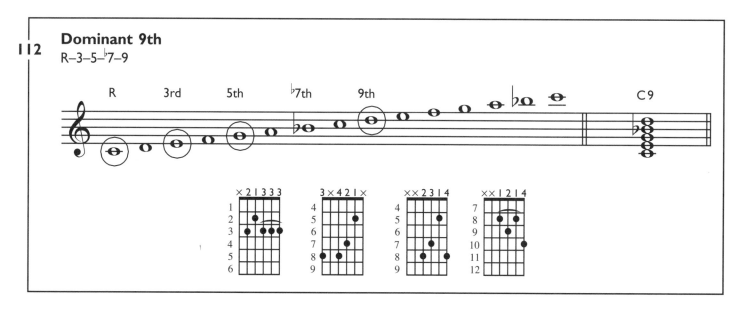

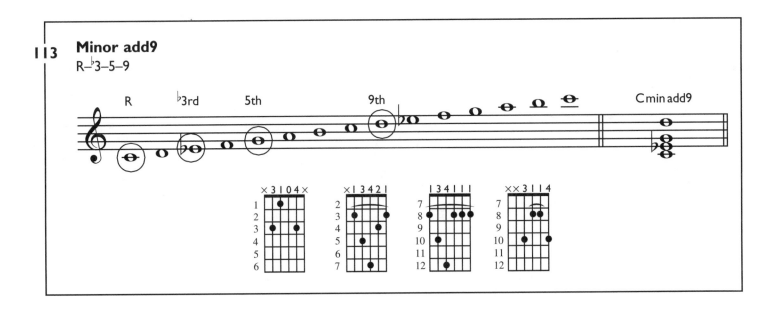

113 **Minor add9**
R–♭3–5–9

114 **Minor 9th**
R–♭3–5–♭7–9

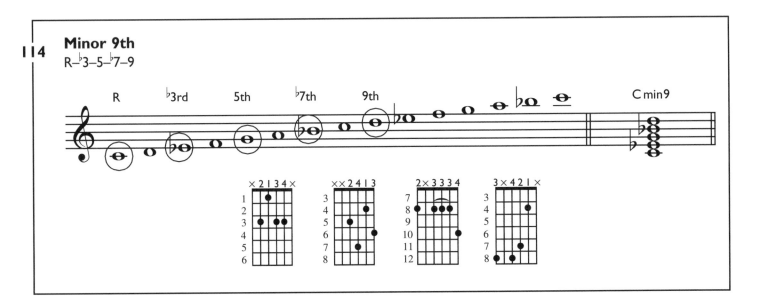

11TH CHORDS

115 **Dominant 11th**
R–3–5–♭7–9–11

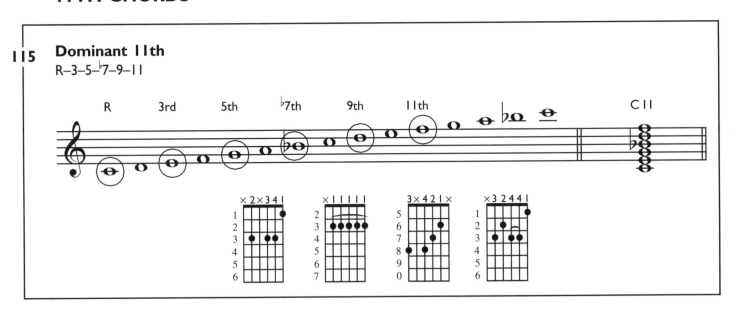

116 Minor 11th
R–♭3–5–♭7–11

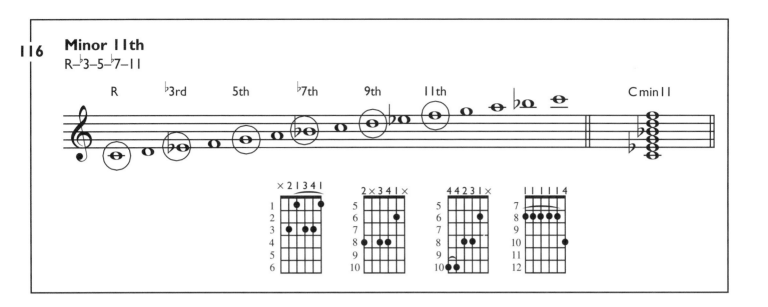

13TH CHORDS

117 Major 13th
R–3–5–7–9–13

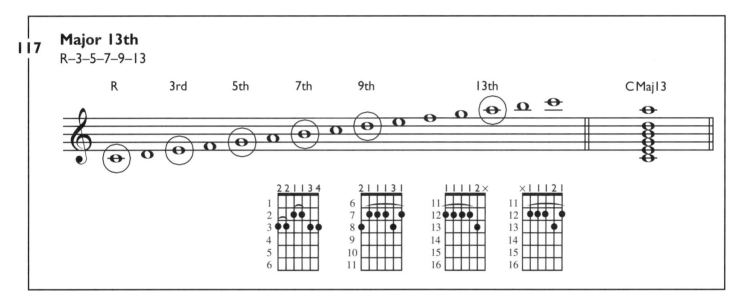

118 Dominant 13th
R–3–5–♭7–9–13

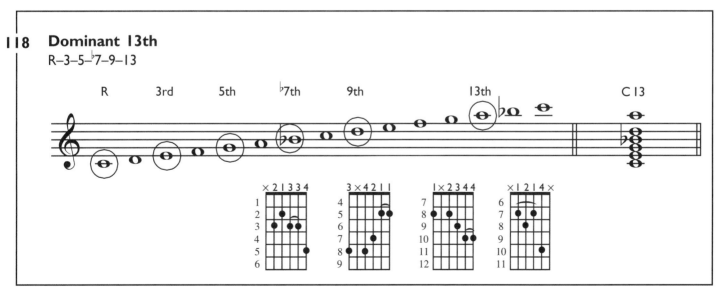

Minor 13th

119 R–♭3–5–♭7–9–13

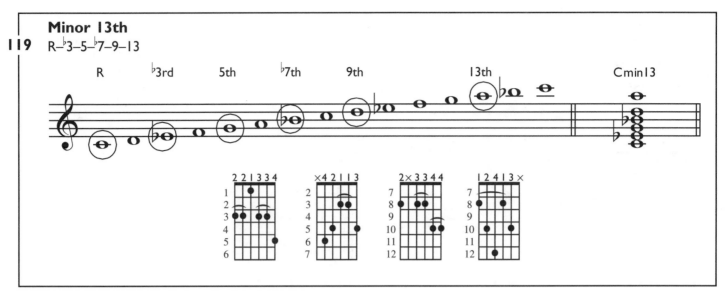

If you want to explore these types of chords even further, check out my book *Jazz Guitar Harmony* published by the National Guitar Workshop and Alfred.

Here's your chance to play a chord progression all over the fretboard and on various string sets. The chords shown are all 7th chords. Try to add extensions wherever you can. Practice playing this progression in the following ways:

1. From the 1st fret through the 5th fret

2. From the 5th fret through the 9th fret

3. From the 8th fret through the 12fth fret

4. On string set 6–5–4–3

5. On string set 5–4–3–2

6. On string set 4–3–2–1

This can be tricky the first time. Be prepared to spend some time on it.

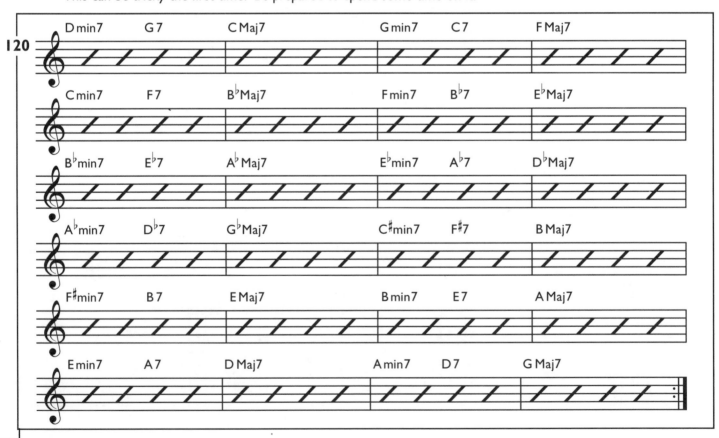

LEARNING TO PLAY DIFFICULT CHORDS

Here are two ideas that should help you learn difficult (or "stretchy") chords.

1. Many people are not very conscious about where their thumb is placed—especially when learning a new chord. Sometimes just moving your thumb to a different location behind the neck can make all the difference. Also, try "relaxing" into the chord. Almost everyone presses way too hard when learning a new chord. Remember how hard you worked on learning your first barre chords? After a while, you realized that it really didn't take that much physical pressure. It's mostly about the balance between wrist and hand position, finger and thumb position and pressure.

2. Try placing your fingers on any chord you find difficult. Sound the strings, checking to make sure all the strings that are supposed to be ringing actually are. Now hold the chord for at least 30 seconds. Then release. Repeat as often as you like. The act of holding the position increases strength and teaches the muscles in your hand and fingers what you want them to do. Most folks just press and release over and over until they eventually learn the chord. Stretching and holding accelerates the whole process.

LEARNING TO SWITCH CHORDS EASILY

The reason some players take a long time to learn to switch between certain chords is because they only have a vague idea of where their fingers are supposed to go. Dissect the entire action finger by finger and you will learn to switch chords much more easily. Take a look at what your 1st finger is required to do during any chord change. Practice moving just that one finger back and forth from where it was on the first chord to where it is supposed to go on the second chord. Follow suit with the remaining fingers.

The next step requires playing the first chord and letting it sustain for four beats—then switch to the second chord, letting it sustain for the same period of time. Don't try to practice this any faster than you can play it correctly. The fingers should move in an "up, over and down" motion. When this starts to feel a little easier cut the time down to just two beats per chord, then one and then possibly eighth notes.

This way of practicing should help you learn the switch faster and when you do, you'll find you're playing "cleaner" than ever as well.

PRACTICING SONGS

When you first sit down to master a song that you (or someone else) has arranged, it is probably a good idea to play through the entire piece a few times. The purpose of this is to get a general idea of what the song's particular issues will be. This is the time to check out things like range, tempo, key (and key changes) and form. After the initial "once over" you are ready to dig in and absorb all of the individual moves that are required in the tune.

To start with, practice the very first move. This could a note going to a chord, a chord going to another chord, a couple of single notes, or any combination—it really doesn't matter. The idea is that you are going to practice that move over and over until it feels easy every time. When you have mastered that much, start working on the very next move the same way—until it feels easy every time. Then practice the two moves together, smoothing it out, making it feel and sound just right. Continue right on through the entire song that way. It may seem like it will take forever but you will progress much faster this way. Here's why:

> There are probably millions of possible moves on a guitar, but a lot of the time we use the same moves over and over from song to song. In the beginning, learning a song this way will take quite a while. The good news is that the next song you work on will probably have several of the same (or same type of) moves in it. Every song you learn will teach you moves that will be found in future songs. Eventually, you will get to the point where you can put together a song pretty quickly. Not practicing this way usually results in sloppy and inconsistent performances.

Once again (and this cannot be emphasized enough), **_you must practice very slowly—never faster than you can play correctly_**.

Following are three tunes to help you work on extended chords. Try to work on the chords, chord changes and the overall arrangement in the ways suggested above.

COURTESY PIERRE BENSUSAN

*Born in 1957, **Pierre Bensusan**, the French-Algerian solo guitarist, blends jazz, classical, Celtic and folk elements. He has been an important figure in expanding the boundaries of solo guitar playing. He is also known for utilizing effects to enhance his solo style.*

FOR THE LOST ONES

HOW COME?

PRAYER

Welcome to the harmonic "spice rack!" If you are accustomed to listening to or playing more commercial kinds of music, you may not yet have been exposed to some of the upcoming sounds. Altered chords add tension and interest to a chord progression. Before we get too deep into the subject at hand, we need to talk about something called *functional harmony*.

Most music is based on a concept known as "tension and release," meaning that during the course of a song, the harmony goes through phases of some *dissonance* (clashing, tense) followed by relative *consonance* (harmonious). This is what keeps a chord progression interesting to the listener. It is generally accepted that the *I* chord in key is the most consonant. The other chords in the key have varying levels of tension, but the trait they have in common is that they all "want" to progress to other chords. All chords, however, are not created equal. Some chords in the key have very strong tendencies and some do not.

Here is a chart that illustrates the most common chord movements.

Chord	Attraction
I	Establishes key center
ii	Moves to *V7* or ♭*ii*
iii	Moves to *vi* or ♭*iii*
IV	Moves to *V7* or *I*
V7	Moves to *I*
vi	Moves to *ii* or ♭*vi*
vii	Moves to *I*

The chord that has the strongest attraction to the *I* chord is *V7*. Play a G7 chord. It practically begs to be followed by *I* (C). This is the basic idea behind tension and release.

Some folks think the *V7* chord isn't filled with quite enough tension. This is where altered dominant chords come into the picture. By altering the 5ths and 9ths of dominant chords we can create much more tension. We alter a tone by either lowering or raising it a half step. Some of the possibilities this creates are shown in the following chart. We'll use G as the root.

G7♭5
G7♯5
G7♭9
G7♯9

We can also combine alterations:

G7♭5♭9
G7♯5♯9
G7♭5♯9
G7♯5♭9

There are other possibilities as well. We can add natural 9ths to chords with altered 5ths. We can also add 13ths to some of these chords, as in G13$\flat$9. Adding $\sharp$11ths to chords is common but it is good to remember that a $\sharp$11 is the same as a $\flat$5 (one octave higher). If you wanted to play a dominant chord with both a $\sharp$5 and a $\flat$5, you could think of this as being a $\flat$5$\flat$13 chord because the $\flat$13 is the same as a $\sharp$5 or $\flat$6.

These chords are used in place of dominant 7th or extended chords. You can experiment freely but it is important to make sure that any alterations you make in the chord do not clash with notes in the melody.

If this is your first excursion into these sounds, you may find some of them a little strange at first. Just keep practicing and trying to use them in your arrangements. For some, altered chords are an acquired taste. They simply don't appear in some musical styles. Jazz, on the other hand, is full of them.

Altered major chords, such as Maj7$\sharp$5, Maj7$\flat$5 and Maj7$\sharp$11, do exist but are not as extensively used. Min7$\flat$5 chords, are part of the diatonic family, while min7$\sharp$5 are used much less often.

The following pages show formulas and fingerings of common altered chords. Practice them and put them to work!

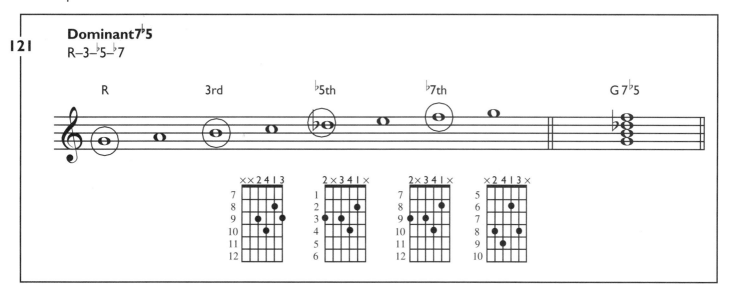

121 **Dominant7$\flat$5**
R–3–$\flat$5–$\flat$7

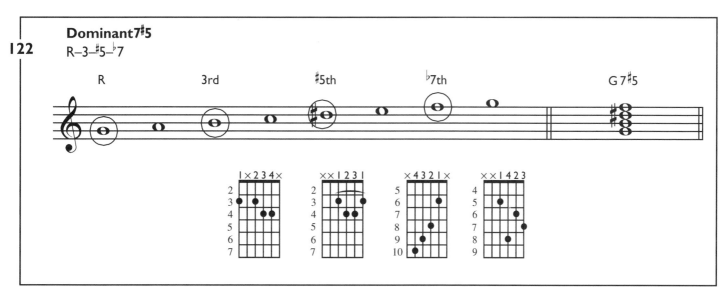

122 **Dominant7$\sharp$5**
R–3–$\sharp$5–$\flat$7

Dominant7♭9

123 R–3–5–♭7–♭9

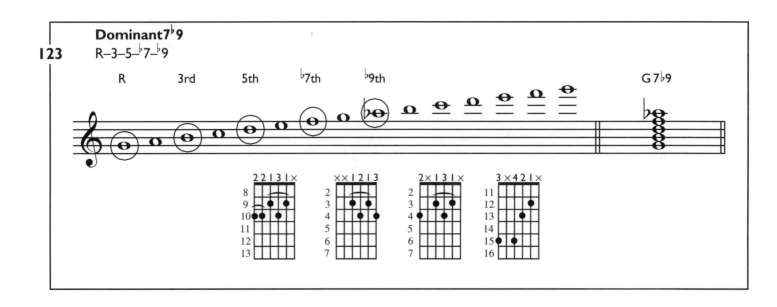

Dominant7♯9

124 R–3–5–♭7–♯9

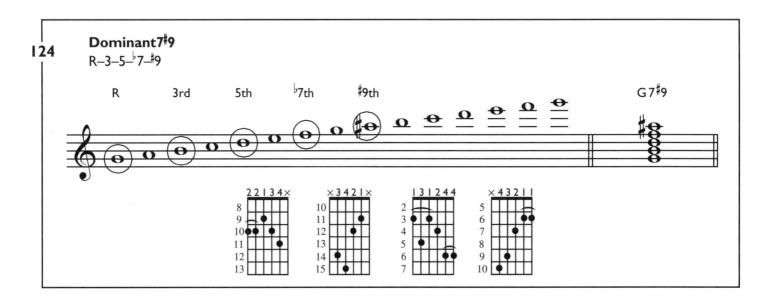

Dominant7♭5♭9

125 R–3–♭5–♭7–♭9

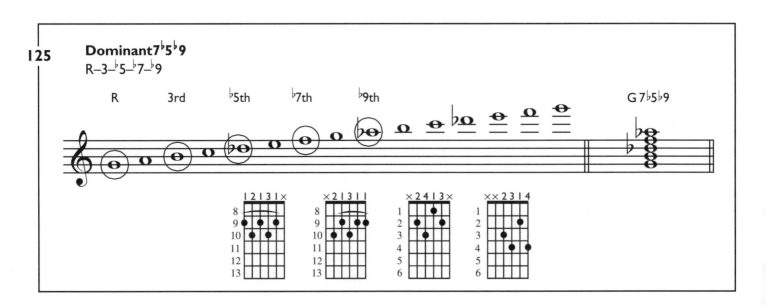

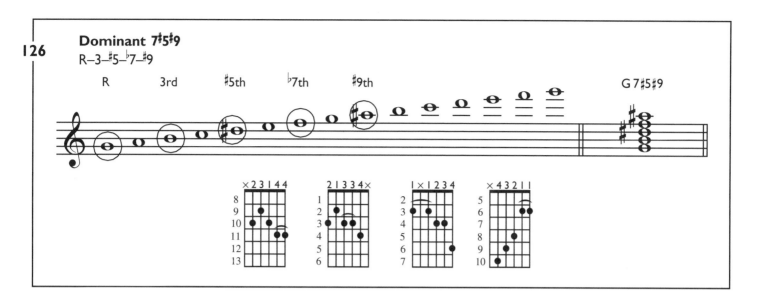

126 **Dominant 7♯5♯9**
R–3–♯5–♭7–♯9

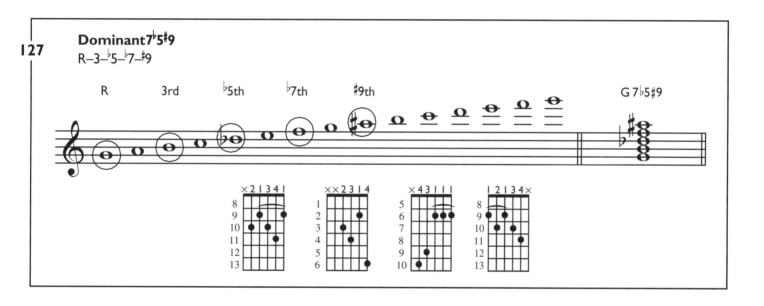

127 **Dominant 7♭5♯9**
R–3–♭5–♭7–♯9

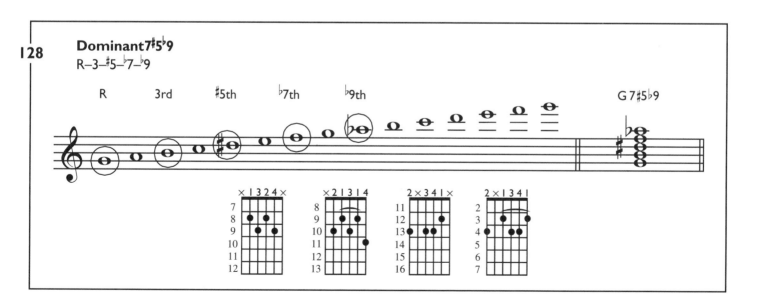

128 **Dominant 7♯5♭9**
R–3–♯5–♭7–♭9

129
Major7#5
R–3–#5–7

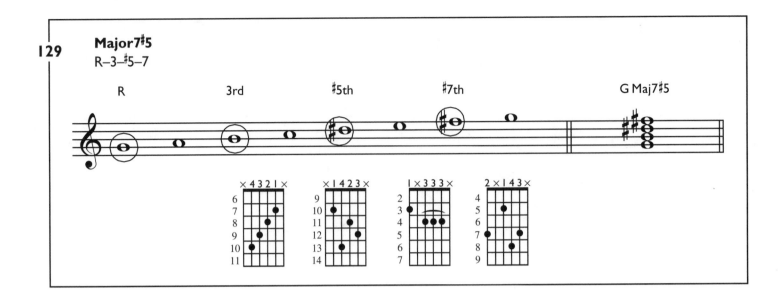

130
Major7♭5
R–3–♭5–7

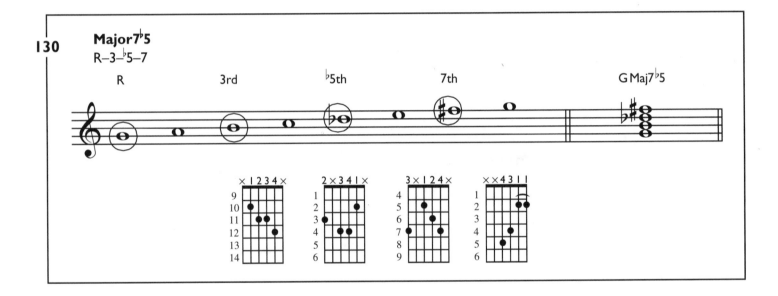

131
Major7#11
R–3–5–7–#11
The 9th is commonly added to this chord as well.

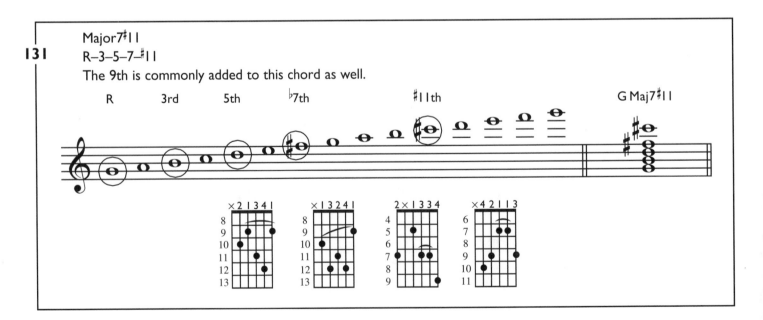

132

Minor7#5
R–♭3–#5–♭7

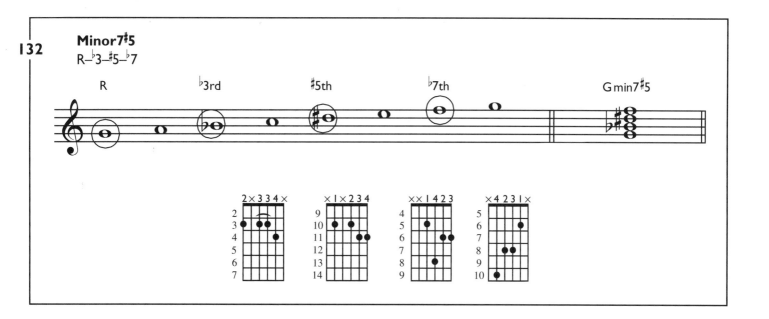

133

Minor7♭5
R–♭3–♭5–♭7

This chord is both altered and diatonic because, as you know, it appears as the *vii* chord in all major keys.

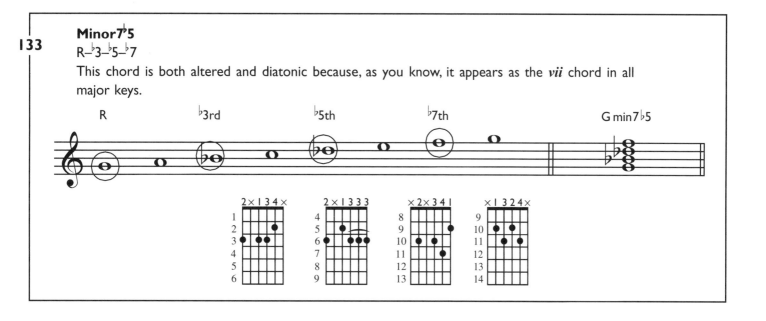

CASA LOMA

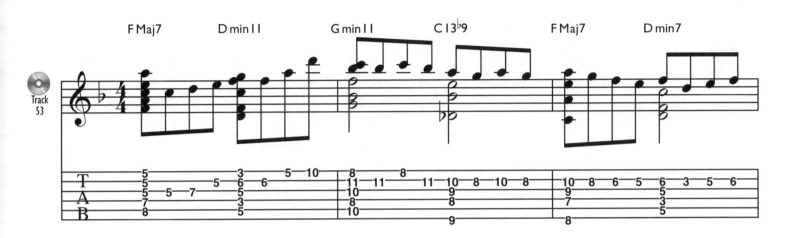

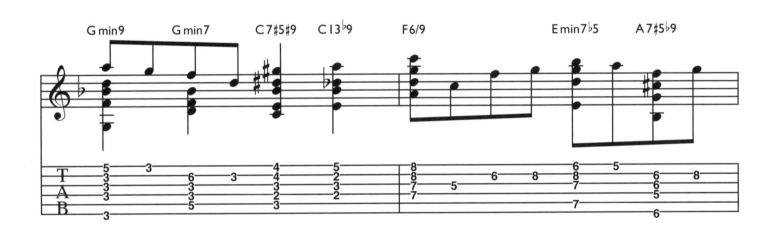

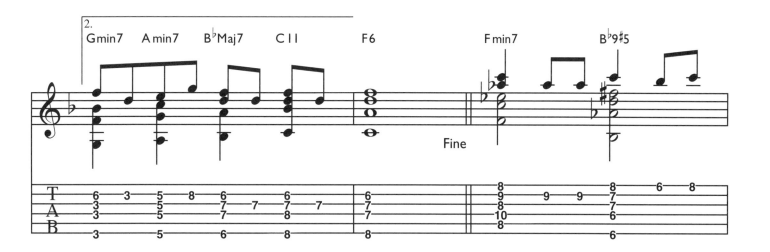

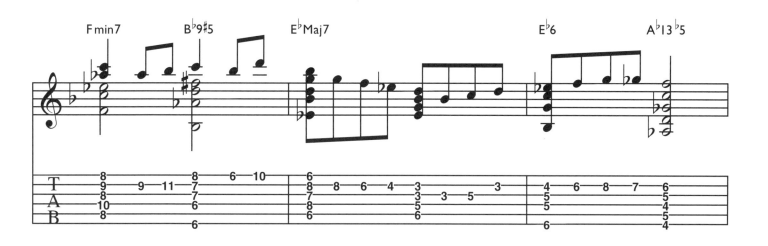

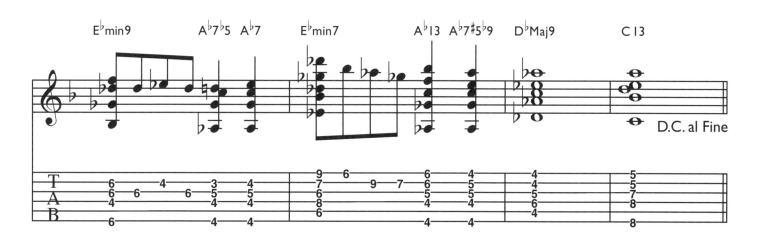

SO LONG, THAT'S ALL FOR NOW

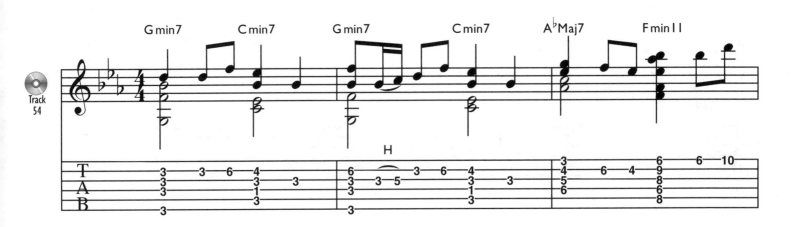

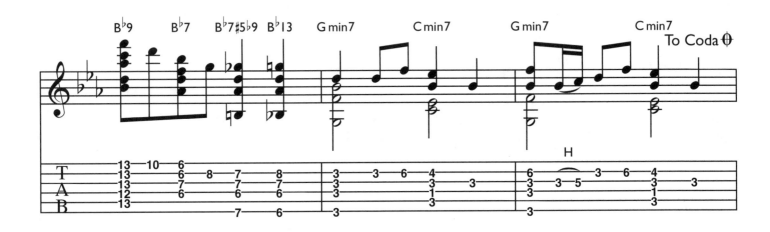

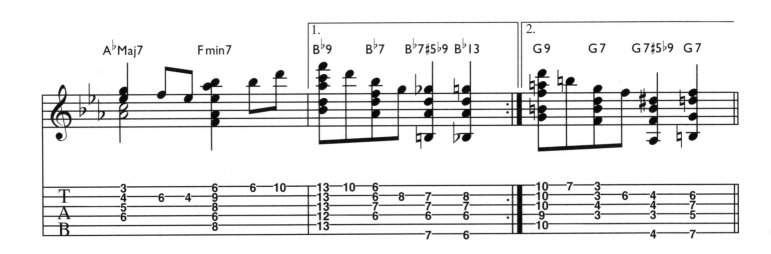